Creating Customer Loyalty

GW00729071

INTRODUCING THE SERIES

Management Action Guides consists of a series of books written in an Open Learning style which are designed to be

- user friendly
- job related

Open Learning text is written in language which is easy to understand and avoids the use of jargon that is usually a feature of management studies. The text is interactive and is interspersed with Action Point questions to encourage the reader to apply the ideas from the text to their own particular situation at work. Space has been left after each Action Point question where responses can be written.

The Management Action Guides series will appeal to people who are already employed in a supervisory or managerial position and are looking to root their practical experience within more formal management studies.

Although Management Action Guides is a series of books that cover all aspects of management education, each book is designed to be free standing and does not assume that the reader has worked through any other book in the series.

Titles in The Management Action Guides series are

    Planning and Managing Change

    Handling Conflict and Negotiation

    Making Effective Presentations

    Managing People and Employee Relations

    Achieving Goals Through Teamwork

    Creating Customer Loyalty

COLLEGE OF MARKETING LIBRARY AND DESIGN

Creating Customer Loyalty

First published in 1992 as *Customers, Competition and Choice* by Manchester Open Learning, Lower Hardman Street, Manchester M3 3FP

This edition published in 1993 by Kogan Page Ltd

Apart from any fair dealing for the purposes of research or private study, or criticism or review, as permitted under the Copyright, Designs and Patents Act, 1988, this publication may only be reproduced, stored or transmitted, in any form or by any means, with the prior permission in writing of the publishers, or in the case of reprographic reproduction in accordance with the terms of licences issued by the Copyright Licensing Agency. Enquiries concerning reproduction outside those terms should be sent to the publishers at the undermentioned address:

Kogan Page Limited
120 Pentonville Road
London N1 9JN

© Manchester Open Learning, 1992, 1993

British Library Cataloguing in Publication Data

A CIP record for this book is available from the British Library.

ISBN 0 7494 1139 2

Printed and bound in Great Britain by Biddles Ltd, Guildford and Kings Lynn

Contents

GENERAL INTRODUCTION

Customers are becoming increasingly important in the lives of most organisations as competition increases. Customers are now presented with more choice than ever before; and this represents a considerable shift of power away from producers to consumers. A number of factors have combined to bring about this change

■ **Deregulation**: the withdrawal of controls and privileges which protected a number of industries from effective competition and put other industries under direct government control.

Privatisation has been only a minor element in this change, although it has been the most visible. In the last decade road transport (both freight and passenger), financial services, air transport, radio broadcasting and telecommunications have all been opened up to competition, with or without privatisation of public corporations. This trend has been common to nearly all developed countries, regardless of the political complexion of their governments

■ **Globalisation**: companies are increasingly viewing the whole world as their potential market, and pressing their governments to remove whatever barriers still exist to international trade. Many large companies have, in effect, lost their original national identities and have become completely internationalised. They are managed from a number of different centres, and produce and sell their products anywhere in the world. Competition and choice is coming from more places than ever before

■ **Technology**: on the production side, modern technology has been applied in three main areas – in production processes, in the products themselves, and in communication systems. The resulting effects for the consumers have been: an increasing variety of goods to choose from, a steady reduction in the prices of what were traditionally 'luxury goods', and a greater awareness of what is available together with better access to it

■ **Rising Standards**: at least for the majority of people in this country, rising real income means that a larger proportion of their income is available for them to use how they choose. Rising standards of living have led people to expect rising standards of quality and service. Typically they want better rather than more

1 CUSTOMERS AND CLIENTS

The terms **customer** and **client** have traditionally been used to describe very different kinds of relationships, but along with the many other changes which we have just described, the distinction between customer and client has become blurred. In fact, it is no longer possible to maintain a clear distinction between the two.

It used to be the case that commercial organisations had customers, and professional and public service organisations had clients. The word 'customer' implied that the relationship was one of straightforward exchange between a buyer and a producer. The word 'client' implied that the provider had some superior professional knowledge, and was is some way 'licensed to practise'. This privileged position of the provider (the professional) carried with it certain obligations to maintain high standards of work and ethics, and to act in the best interests of the client. The client had relatively less power than the customer; and the professional and public service provider had correspondingly more responsibility than the commercial producer.

This neat distinction is breaking down from both ends. In the professional/client relationship the client is becoming more like the traditional idea of a customer. In the producer/customer relationship the producers are becoming increasingly professional, in the sense of responding to the particular needs of individuals.

In the old professions the traditional distance between the professional and the client is disappearing. Better educated and more assertive clients expect to be kept informed of what is being done for them, and want to share in the decisions that are going to affect their lives. For example, patients are 'repossessing' their own bodies and their own teeth and getting into a dialogue with their doctors and dentists about treatment.

In the public services it is current policy to put more power and choice into the hands of the users. There is political debate about whether it is being done appropriately in some public services; but the general principle that the balance of power should be tipped in favour of the clients/users/customers of public services is common ground for all parties.

1.1 GOODS AND SERVICES

Meanwhile, in the commercial world, the service sector is growing much faster than manufacturing, and the distinction between goods and services is breaking down. Increasingly the producers of tangible goods are obliged to compete on the quality of their services. The tangible item becomes just one element of a more comprehensive package. Personal computers, for example, are now so much alike in their physical appearance and performance that their makers compete mainly on installation services, maintenance and replacement, upgrades, manuals and training, customisation, advice, and 'hot–lines'. Manufacturers of radiators, fans and trunking find themselves drawn into designing and installing heating and air conditioning systems because that is the only way of making themselves different from the rest. It also brings them into contact with the ultimate customer and 'real need', which is for heating and comfort not for tubes and fans.

This tendency for goods to become services means that customers increasingly have to trust their suppliers and rely upon their reputation and integrity, because they cannot assess what they are getting until after they have bought it. If you are simply buying personal computers you can check their specifications and inspect them in the showroom, and you will know what you are getting before you commit yourself. If, on the other hand you are buying personal computers, plus a network design, plus installation, plus advice on software, plus a maintenance contract, you will be interested as much in the quality of the people as the quality of the hardware. In other words, you will expect something that resembles the old professional/client relationship rather more than it resembles the old supplier/customer. In the rest of this book we shall use the simple word **customer** at all times, to cover customers, clients, purchasers, patients, passengers, punters, and all the other rich variety of words used to describe the people at the receiving end of goods and services.

1.2 CUSTOMERS AS PART OF THE BUSINESS

Whenever you hear the old cliche 'the customer is always right' you probably assume that it is being used ironically. You may also have seen the popular poster which shows a lion, with the caption 'The Customer is King'. This image of the customer as a dangerous animal reveals more than its publishers intended.

As a customer yourself, in a variety of different roles, you know that you are not always right, and you are certainly not king. These tired slogans suggest that, as a customer, you expect to be treated with servility and fear. Most customers

ᴍᴛᴏ749 4113921001
658·812

would willingly trade–in that treatment in part exchange for being listened to, being taken seriously and being valued.

You could say that customers are the only real asset that a business has. Without customers there is no business, and none of the other assets have any commercial value. The other assets may have cost a lot but they are not worth anything without customers. Customers, therefore, are a part of the business and not something separate from it. The rest of this book looks at what this implies.

1.3   WHO IS YOUR CUSTOMER?

The parable of the Good Samaritan was a complex answer to a simple question, 'who is my neighbour?'

'Who is my customer?' is another simple question that has no easy answer.

If you are selling a product to a business organisation, is the customer

- the purchasing specialist who negotiates terms and makes the contact?
- the manager who holds the budget which will pay for the product?
- the staff who will be using it?
- the staff who will be maintaining it?
- the person who will decide whether to use your product next time?
- the customers of the person who will be using it?

Clearly, the answer is, 'any or all of them, depending on circumstances'. They form a kind of composite customer with a variety of different interests and concerns. In an ideal world you would want to be able to satisfy all of them. In practice there may have to be trade–offs among competing requirements.

It is very unlikely that all of these interested parties will be involved in the initial decision on what to buy. Some may not even have been considered or consulted by the principal decision makers. Nonetheless they are part of your constituency. You have a professional responsibility to consider the interests of this wider circle of customers, whether or not your immediate client expects you to do so.

ACTION POINT 1

Who is your customer? List as many people as you can who could be described as 'your customer'.

How many of the different types of customer you wish to take into account, and how much weight you attach to their interests and opinions, will depend on a number of factors. For example

- the scale of your operation
- the expected life of your product
- its relative impact on people's lives
- its visibility
- the consequences of failure or breakdown

If you were selling boxes of chocolates, for example, you could probably afford to take a narrow view of your customers, as the people who pay the money. However, this narrow view would be indefensible if you were selling anything that had a strong impact on the lives of people who were not parties to the formal contract. They will think of themselves as your customers, even if you do not. Sooner or later they will make sure that you take notice of them.

Who were the customers of the companies who designed and built those blocks of flats put up in the 60s to be knocked down in the 80s, when even the homeless refused to live in them? Whoever they were, they were not the people who were going to live in them, or the people who were going to share their urban environment with them.

If these building projects are now regarded by town planners and architects as 'experiments which failed', this is an expensive way of discovering with hindsight what all the prospective occupiers and users could have told them at the time. But no one asked them, because they were not perceived as the customers.

So, if the customer has many faces and many interests, what is the customer buying?

CHAPTER SUMMARY

Having completed this chapter you should now

■ know the difference between goods and services

■ understand the importance of the customer in today's competitive environment

■ be able to define the meaning of customer in the various forms it can take

■ understand what types of customer requirements can exist

If you are unsure about any of these areas, go back and re-read the relevant part(s) of the text.

2 WHAT IS YOUR PRODUCT?

If we ask the question 'what is your product?' Your first reply might be another question. 'Do you mean what I personally produce, or the end product which my organisation supplies to the customer?' As we shall see later this distinction is not as clear as it sounds; but for the present let us consider the product.

2.1 THE PHYSICAL PRODUCT

The temptation is always to reply in terms of the physical features of the product; as for example: light bulbs, packing cases, computer work–stations, hamburgers and fries. The producer's concepts of their product is typically what it **is**, whereas the customer's interest in the product is in what it **does**.

2.2 THE BENEFITS OF THE PRODUCT

With the possible exception of works of art customers rarely wish to possess something for the sake of its history, construction, materials or physical features. What moves the customer is the benefit which it can deliver. It is not what is but what it does that the customer is buying. Salespeople typically use the words features and benefits to describe the distinction which we are making. A product feature which cannot be related to some corresponding benefit is of no interest to the customer. It is probably best not even to mention it, because it reminds the customer that you are, in effect, charging them for something they do not want

- the customer does not want 5 mm drills, they want 5 mm holes

- they do not want packing cases, they want safe storage and transport of their goods. They may also, for example want them to be immediately recognisable

- they don't want track lighting with (adjustable) spots and floods. They want to be able to see what they are doing, without glare or eyestrain, and to match the level of brightness to the way their room is being used

- they do not want three hours in the train, they want to be at their destination

Here is a typically American statement of the point we are making.

Don't sell me clothes. Sell me a sharp appearance, style, and attractiveness.

Don't sell me insurance. Sell me peace of mind and a great future for my family and me.

Don't sell me a house. Sell me comfort, contentment, a good investment, and pride of ownership.

Don't sell me books. Sell me pleasant hours and the profits of knowledge.

Don't sell me toys. Sell my children happy moments.

Don't sell me a computer. Sell me the pleasures and profits of the miracles of modern technology.

Don't sell me tyres. Sell me freedom from worry and low cost per mile.

Don't sell me airline tickets. Sell me a fast, safe, on-time arrival at my destination feeling like a million dollars.

Don't sell me *things*. Sell me ideals, feelings, self-respect, home life, and happiness.

Please don't sell me *things*.

Here is a more restrained British example of an advertisement for computer software which makes direct use of the features/benefits relationship.

Features	Benefits
Popular Page Layout Options	
Multiple Columns	Enhance your documents with multi-column layouts.
Direct Graphics	Easily insert graphics from MacPaint, MacDraw, Claris CAD and File Insertion other graphics applications using MacPaint, PICT, or TIFF file formats.
Precision Formatting	Achieve your desired layout with format options in points, picas, inches, or centimetres. Precisely set line spacing in 0.25 point increments, and include automatic space after or before a paragraph.

Left/Right Page Formats	Design speciality layouts by selecting left and right page formats, along with left and right headers and footers.
Page Views	View and edit entire pages with reduced size and side-by-side features.
Additional Style Features	Create emphasis with double underline, strike through, or use of colour styles.

Powerful Document Productivity Tools

Mail Merge	Quickly generate form letters, reports, and lists by accessing selected data from FileMaker Pro or other database, text, and spreadsheet files
Comprehensive Find/Change	Make comprehensive changes with powerful search and replace capability for locating and changing text by any combination of word, phrase, font size, and style.
Spelling Checker	Correct your spelling as you work using the 100,000-word dictionary.
Thesaurus	Communicate more precisely by selecting words from the 660,000- synonym on-line thesaurus.
Footnotes/Endnotes	Create professional documentation with your choice of automatic or user-specific numbering and formatting.
Foreign Language Dictionaries	Check foreign language spelling with additional dictionaries, including French, German, and Spanish.

ACTION POINT 2

Identify six features of your own product and translate them into benefits.

This way of thinking about your product is obviously more than just a mental discipline. It is the foundation of all discussion with the customer, and it also provides the link between the external market–related activities of the business and the internal production–related activities.

2.3 TOTAL QUALITY MANAGEMENT

Many companies are now adopting the principles of Total Quality Management (TQM) as their guiding light in managing their production. The fundamental definition of quality enshrined in all the texts on **TQM** is **quality is fitness for use.** This idea that quality is dependent upon use brings the customer into the picture, because it is the customer who decides the use. This had led some people to reword the definition, to make the link with the customer even more obvious **quality is what the customers says it is**.

So, even if you have no personal contact with the external customers of your organisation, and if what you are doing or making is consumed entirely within the organisation, the customer still enters into your work in at least two ways.

Firstly, whatever you produce must be used by somebody and that somebody is therefore your customer.

Secondly, there has to be an unbroken chain of consequences that links your output with the external customer.

ACTION POINT 3

How does your company discover your customers' definition of quality?

CHAPTER SUMMARY

Having completed this chapter you should now

■ know the difference between goods and services

■ understand the importance of the customer in today's competitive environment

If you are unsure about any of these areas, go back and re-read the relevant part(s) of the text.

3 THE INTERNAL CUSTOMER

We have to start by supposing that every activity in an organisation has a purpose. It may not always appear to be so; but this is the essential difference between what we might call recreation in contrast to work. Work delivers some sort of an output, in addition to whatever pleasure of self–fulfilment it might give the performer. And this output, whatever it is, must have a customer.

Two things, at least, must be going on within any organisation.

Firstly, a set of activities which combine to make the end product for the external customer – call it 'production' if you want to be traditional.

Secondly, a set of activities which maintain the resources and abilities of the organisation, and which enable it to continue producing.

The second set of activities has traditionally come under attack from people looking for efficiency. It has been called rude names, like 'overheads' or 'burden' – even by accountants who are very much a part of it themselves.

Production tends to be regarded as a good thing because it is easy to see why it is there and what it is doing. There is a logical FLOW to production which makes it relatively easy to identify a series of stages, and a clear succession of internal suppliers and customers until the end product hits the external customer.

By contrast, if you are in the business of Personnel Management, Financial Accounting, Management Information Systems, Security, Sports and Social Amenities, it is not so immediately evident what is the product and who is the customer. However, you could argue that because the answers are more difficult to find it is even more important to ask the questions. If you do not have a customer you do not have a product, and vice versa. You have no way then of judging the appropriateness of what you are doing, of defining standard and quality, or even of justifying the existence of your job.

3.1 INTERNAL RESTRUCTURING

Over the past decade very few companies have avoided rationalisation, restructuring, or 'shake down'. The Americans coined the word 'downsizing' to describe it. Whatever you call it, the result has invariably been a large reduction in the number of employees. What surprised many people was that, in most cases, this was achieved without any visible deterioration in output. On the contrary, there was often an improvement in the quality of the work done. Indeed, one of the commonest reasons for making these changes was to achieve such improvements.

The overall intention was usually to improve the competitiveness of the organisation, and this cannot be done by indiscriminate cost–cutting. If you have been involved in any of these major slimming exercises you will probably recall that after the initial shock and disbelief, most of the jobs which had disappeared were never missed. Clearly this does not mean that the people who had been doing them were not, in their own way, busy and conscientious. What it invariably means is that what they were producing did not have a customer.

There are many reasons why this situation can come about.

The most obvious one is technical obsolescence; the customer no longer has any use for the product

- maintenance staff standing–by to maintain equipment which no longer breaks down like it used to

- workshop staff who used to recondition components which are now simply thrown away

- telex operators, by–passed by user–operated fax machines

Then there were jobs where the customer didn't really want the product anyway

- inspection functions, whose only apparent output was rejects and recycled work. When their contribution was called into question, it became very clear that no one actually had any use for rejects and reworking. What the supposed customer really wanted was consistency and reliability first time around

- some levels of supervision, whose primary output was the enforcement of the rules, which no one really wanted. The staff wanted to be trusted. The management wanted the staff to use their intelligence and initiative. There was no real demand for rules and their enforcement

Others were focused on activities rather than results

■　typically they were looking to their own colleagues for approval rather than to their customers

■　the training departments who used the number of employee–days of training as a measure of their output, not realising that this was a measure of what they cost the organisation, rather than what they contributed. What the customers wanted was improved performance on the job

■　those computer people who were more excited by the prospect of exploiting the technical capabilities of the equipment, than by the opportunity it offered to put more power into the hand of their customers

Others were misled into treating the boss as the only customer, and were surprised when they and the boss went down together.

ACTION POINT 4

Within your own company how has internal restructuring been managed? Are there any changes which you feel, with hindsight, could have been handled differently?

Apart from a very few jobs, like secretary or personal assistant, every job has its own hard core of purposes which are the personal responsibility of the job–holder, and which do not belong to anyone else. In other words, doing what the boss says can never be the whole of any job. There has to be someone outside that closed system who is being served by it; and that person we have called the customer.

Many employees have fallen into the trap of following the lead of bosses who were not themselves concerned with meeting customer's needs. They may have found favour within their own sections; but viewed from the outside their behaviour often looked more like a self–serving conspiracy.

Long term security for employees, and departments, and for whole organisations, depends upon being useful to their customers. They then have a group of people who need them and will make some effort to ensure their survival if they are under threat.

3.2 WHO IS THE INTERNAL CUSTOMER, WHAT IS THE SERVICE?

Following the logic of our argument, you cannot say what your product is until you have identified your customer; because the product is not a piece of hardware or an activity, but a customer's need satisfied. If this is not a customary way of thinking and talking in your organisation, then it takes an effort of will to rethink your job in these terms. What makes the effort worthwhile is that it highlights the bits of the job that really make a difference.

To show how it works, we will take an example of the Personnel Department of a medium sized company; and look at just three of their customers

Customer	Need	Provision
Staff in General	Fair reward for effort	Evaluation, pay scales relativities
	Recognition for achievement	Appraisal, performance bonus, awards
	Sense of security	Employment, redeployment, redundancy policies
	Competence to do the job	Induction, job-related training
	Support in difficulties	Welfare, counselling, loans
Job applicant	Ability to judge: - would they like the job? - could they do the job?	Job advertisement, information packs for applicants, telephone advice
	Equal opportunity to compete	Application form design, short-listing procedures
	Opportunity to present the best case for themselves	Application forms, interview plans, interviewer training
	Fair selection or rejection	Procedures and criteria for acceptance, feedback to successful and unsuccessful applicants
Top management	Competent workforce	Training programmes, recruitment policies and practices
	Well-controlled labour costs	Grading structures, pay scales, negotiations
	An organisation which is willing to co-operate and to change	Communications, consultation, retraining and job-security policies and practices

Notice that

■ the need in each case is more or less abstract. It is a belief or a feeling that the customer has. For example; recognition, support, or opportunity are not visible or tangible things, they are whatever the customer thinks they are

■ we have used the word 'provision' to stand for the visible activities and outputs of the department. The real product is a satisfied need

■ none of the needs are absolute, you can have more or less of each of them

■ some of them look like they may be in competition with each other

ACTION POINT 5

Now try a similar analysis of your own department or section, using your internal customers if possible. Write in the grid below, and keep to this order.

First. List out the major groupings of customers. There must be more than one. But if you can identify more than about six categories of customer, try to reduce the number by asking the following questions

1   Do some of them have needs so similar that they could be regarded as in the same category?

2   Could you narrow your focus to your own particular bit of your department?

3   Is you department/section trying to do too much?

Second. Put yourself in the position of the customer and consider what needs they look to you to satisfy. What do they expect you to deliver in terms of valued benefits.

Third. For each need you have listed, identify under Provision at least one visible thing which you do or make which satisfies the need.

Customer	Need	Provision

This is much more than an academic exercise in expressing needs in abstract terms. It is a tool for assessing whether what you are doing is relevant and definable, and for identifying the gaps in your own information. Examine your entries in the grid and ask yourself the following questions:

Are there customers without needs?

Is this because you do not know enough about their needs to be able to express them on their behalf? or is it because they have no particular expectations of you, and are therefore not customers after all? Perhaps you are their customer?

Are there any needs without provisions?

A need without provision is a permanent piece of unfinished business. It is a source of tension in any organisation.

Is the customer justified in expecting you to be providing for the need in question? If the answer is **yes**, you have some explaining to do. If the answer is **no**, you have some persuading to do

Are there provisions without needs?

In theory these could not appear on your diagram. So consider whether there are any significant activities which you are engaged in as part of your work that cannot be traced back via a need to a customer. What sort of activities are these? What are they for? Do they come into any of the categories listed above?

3.3 TRACING THE LINK TO THE EXTERNAL CUSTOMER

Jan Carlzon, the Chief Executive of SAS, the Scandinavian airline, achieved a remarkable turnround in the fortunes of his company in the early 80s, by focusing the attention of the whole organisation upon the customer. One of Carlzon's notions was to invert the conventional way of depicting organisation structure.

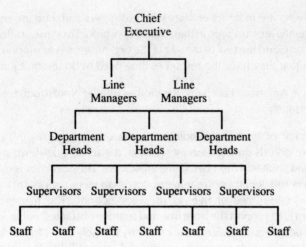

fig 3.1 Conventional organisation structure

This way of visualising a company, showing management on top and staff below, was a perfect expression of the conventional notion that it is the job of management to tell staff what to do and the job of the staff to do what the management tell them. Missing altogether from the picture were the customers.

The alternative view which Carlzon proposed was to put the customers at the top of the structure.

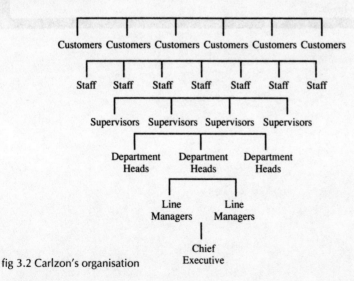

fig 3.2 Carlzon's organisation

The staff who are in direct contact with customers and who are serving their needs directly, are now seen in their rightful position. They are, in effect, leading the company, and the task of the rest of the organisation is to support them, and to ensure that they have the resources they need to do the best job they can.

At least one American company, the clothes retailer Nordstrom, has taken this notion seriously.

The primacy of front-line employees shows up in the organization chart Nordstrom unfurls during training sessions. It's an up-side-down pyramid. At the top, and greatest in number, come customers. The next layer is salespeople, then buyers and department managers, store managers, regional managers, and finally the committee of five, at the very bottom. The manager's job at Nordstrom is to support the front line and remove obstacles, not to issue edicts and push people around. Since the company is highly decentralized, front-line employees enjoy wide ranging authority and responsibility. In contrast to most department stores, where merchandise buyers are czars and salespeople are serfs, sales reps at Nordstrom strongly influence the decisions of buyers. Both buyers and department managers must spend half their time on the selling floor, interacting with customers.

The logical consequence of this view of the business is that all organisational paths lead to the customer. Carlzon's philosophy has been summarised as

'If you are not directly serving the needs of the Customer yourself, then you had better be serving the needs of someone who is.'

ACTION POINT 6

Draw a diagram of your company's management structure and comment on it in the light of the above information.

The reality of most organisations is still a long way from this model, but it does provide a useful template to lay against your organisation and assess whether its energies are being channelled in the right direction. The trick is to trace the chain of consequences which connects your output to the needs of the external customer, using the least number of links. The process is useful for identifying weak links and 'broken chains', ie. chains which stop short of making the connection with the external customer.

Here is an example of an attempt to track the chain of consequences for one of the outputs of a management accounting job.

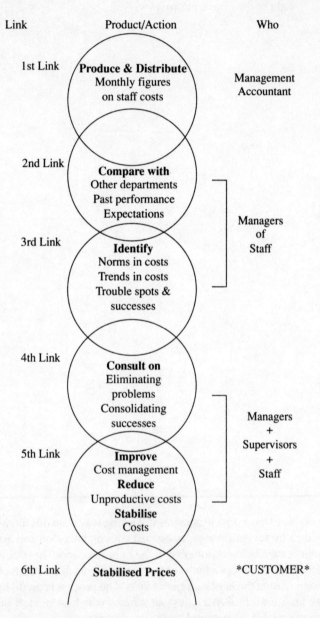

Link	Product/Action	Who
1st Link	**Produce & Distribute** Monthly figures on staff costs	Management Accountant
2nd Link	**Compare with** Other departments Past performance Expectations	Managers of Staff
3rd Link	**Identify** Norms in costs Trends in costs Trouble spots & successes	
4th Link	**Consult on** Eliminating problems Consolidating successes	Managers + Supervisors + Staff
5th Link	**Improve** Cost management **Reduce** Unproductive costs **Stabilise** Costs	
6th Link	**Stabilised Prices**	*CUSTOMER*

fig 3.3 Chain of consequences

It is clear from this analysis that the best contribution which the Management Accountant can make to the external customer is to make it easy for his internal customers to forge links 2 and 3, and to ensure at least that the chain does not break at those points.

ACTION POINT 7

Take at least one of your products which goes to an internal customer and trace a chain of consequences which finally produce value for the external customer.

Alternatively, if you are primarily serving the external customer directly, use an example from another department whose work you know.

3.4 GETTING ALONGSIDE YOUR INTERNAL CUSTOMERS

According to Peter Drucker, probably the most influential management theorist of this century, 'the purpose of a business is to create and retain customers'. We have in effect extended this proposition to cover not only businesses as a whole, but also departments within them, and even individual jobs. We all have customers; our customers have customers and so on, in an unbroken chain which extends from the centre of the business right through to the external customer and the final user.

Up to now we have emphasised the essential similarity between the internal and the external customers. But clearly there is still a fairly obvious and important difference, which is that

> the relationships with the internal customers are subordinate to the need to serve the external customer.

So you and your internal customers have to conduct your affairs with at least one eye on the over–riding purpose of the whole business. This common purpose, which unites the customers and the providers within the organisation, means that you are not in the business of simply giving your internal customers what they want. You have to satisfy yourself that what they say they want is relevant to the purpose of the business you are in. You are responsible for the consequences of your actions; and ignorance is no excuse.

All of this means that there has to be openness, exchange and discussion among the various parts of the organisation. It is no longer a matter of one department giving the orders to another one, but rather a matter of both of them coming to an agreement on how they will jointly contribute to the common purpose.

The word **partnership** is being used in more and more companies to describe the nature of the relationship that they want to encourage among their departments. The word is well chosen because it implies

- a common cause
- a relationship of equality
- acceptance of mutual dependence
- discussion
- agreement
- shared responsibility

This description of partnership often sounds hopelessly optimistic to people who have grown up with inter–departmental rivalries, buck–passing, blame allocation, one–upmanship and name calling. All of these are frequently mistaken for team spirit and even for high morale, but in reality they are costly games played at the customer's expense.

> 'I can't find anyone in accounts who knows about your refund, so I can't tell you why it hasn't been paid, leave this one with me'.
>
> 'I don't care if you did promise it for Friday, we're working flat out already and there's no way we can fit it in. You'll have to go back and talk yourself out of it'.
>
> 'I'm afraid stores aren't answering their phone at the moment, so I can't tell you yet whether we can replace it or not'.
>
> 'I am confident that the studio is definitely available. I can't tell you for sure whether a technician will be free for that week; that comes under Tech Services. The cost, of course, will depend on whether it includes our technician or whether you have to bring your own; but in any case that comes under Rates and Quotes. You had better phone them on extension 7533. If you want a car park pass, Security won't issue one on my authority. It will probably be easiest if you contact them direct and explain your position. They are on .....'.

If any of these scenes sound even vaguely familiar, you will know what it feels like when companies make their own internal structures, communication problems and rivalries into the customer's problem.

The customer does not want to know. If they have any choice they will take their business somewhere else.

Increasingly they do have a choice; and that is why more and more companies have started to look at themselves from the external customer's point of view and ask

■ are we looking after ourselves at the expense of the customer?

■ are we relying upon the customer to make our own system work?

■ are we making our problems the customer's problems?

■ are we using the customer as a weapon against other departments?

If the answer to any of these questions is YES, it is a strong signal that partnership is lacking. Partnership is not necessarily a formal arrangement, with meetings and agendas and reports; although it may work in this way. More importantly, it is an attitude of mind. By focusing on the effect you are having on the customer you put your internal relationships into a new perspective. 'Keeping the customer' is a game where everyone wins. 'Maintaining internal privileges and rivalries' is a game with winners and losers, but usually more losers than winners because the customer is one of them.

ACTION POINT 8

Within your own organisation identify

a) Who is your internal customer?

b) Whose internal customer are you?

3.5   STAFF AS CUSTOMERS

You will recall the proposition, which we credited to Jan Carlzon: if our business is to be driven by the needs of the external customers, then the people who are in direct contact with the customer should be positioned 'at the top' and the rest of the organisation should be serving their needs.

If we accept this argument it leads to the interesting conclusion that the staff are in some sense the customers of the management.

The point which Carlzon was trying to emphasise was that the people who are closest to the customer usually have the best and most reliable information about the customer's needs; and that, as far as the customer is concerned, they are the company. It is sensible, therefore, for managers and supervisors to listen to what the 'front line' staff have to say, and to ensure that they have the authority and resources to respond sensibly to the customer's needs. 'Sensibly' in this case, means in a way which seems sensible to the customer.

When staff are unable to satisfy a customer's request they need to be able to offer a better explanation than 'it's the rules' or I'm not allowed to ...' or best, of all, 'it's more than my job's worth'.

Staff forced to confess their own powerlessness in this way are being punished twice over; once by their boss who has denied them the power and the information they need, and once more by the customer, who is likely to dump their frustration on the defenceless staff member.

So, to give service, the staff need to be trusted, they need to be given power, and they need to understand the intentions that lie behind the rules of the job.

All this translates into the first rule of customer service.

> **Your staff will not treat the customers any better than they are treated themselves.**

This rule corresponds quite closely with most people's experience as employees and as customers. But it is more than just a plausible generalisation from common experience; it has, in fact, been verified by a number of independent research projects. These have all shown a strong relationship between the way the customers describe the style and quality of the service and the way the staff describe the style and quality of the management and supervision which they receive.

It is fairly easy to demonstrate this relationship for businesses which have a high element of service and personal contact in their products. But it is one of the important discoveries of the last twenty years, that the relationship is equally strong in manufactured goods. The quality of the management and supervision, the effectiveness of the training, and the extent to which the staff are listened to and involved in problem–solving, are all directly reflected in the quality and reliability of the product. They are therefore all visible to the customer. The superiority of the Toyota car over, say, the Lada is only partly a consequence of superior equipment and technology. It is just as much a measure of the commitment of the workers and the extent to which their knowledge and intelligence has been cultivated by their management.

In the 1980s Jaguar Motors achieved a notable turnaround. They re-established their damaged reputation for quality, and reinstated themselves in markets which they had almost lost beyond recall. There was obviously plenty of room for improvement, and changes were made in every area of operation. But the biggest single change, which enabled all the others to work, was what they have come to call the culture change. This was nothing other than a new willingness to listen to the customers and take their views seriously; and the mirror–image of this within the company – a willingness to listen to staff and to use their experience.

ACTION POINT 9

Show, in diagrammatical form, your position in the chain of internal customers which leads to your external customers.

3.6 SERIOUS CONSEQUENCES

Focusing the attention of the company on the customer leads to some inevitable consequences in the way the company manages its own internal affairs.

1   To ensure that each department and individual is doing the right thing, they need to make sure that they are linking up together, and that all their links connect them ultimately to the customer.

2   To ensure that each department is doing things right, they need to

   ■   use their staff's experience and insight

   ■   provide them with the information and resources they need to give good service and solve problems

The first is about **effectiveness** and the second is about **efficiency**.

At this point you may well be thinking: 'If it is that simple, and if the potential pay–off is so great, why isn't everyone doing it?'

There are several answers to that question

■   it may be simple, but it isn't easy

■   it supposes that companies really believe that 'the purpose of their business is to create and keep customers'. It is very easy for companies to pay lip–service to this ideal, while, in fact, they are pursuing something entirely different. Management are sometimes carried away by their own public relations, and forget that talking about it is not the same as doing it

■   it requires managers and supervisors to exercise skills of listening and trusting, and to surrender some of their personal power and control to colleagues and staff. Many of them would rather not do that if it could be avoided

■   they may be doing quite nicely without it. If there is no effective competition, and if the customers are completely docile, then there is very little pressure to listen and respond, or to develop and innovate

CHAPTER SUMMARY

Having completed this chapter you should now

■   understand the reasons for rationalisation in companies

■   be aware of the concept of the internal customer

■   know what is meant by a need without provision

■   see the importance of the external customer to the whole of a company's operations

■   realise the need to treat internal and external customers with equal deference

If you are unsure about any of these areas, go back and re-read the relevant part(s) of the text.

4 FINDING OUT WHAT THE CUSTOMER NEEDS

There is often a great deal of assuming and guessing going on in service organizations about the customer's attitudes and habits. It is common for those who run service organizations to form their views of the customers through long years of experience but with little actual data. Each manager has a theory about what is important to the customer, but in relatively few cases is this theory actually grounded in reasonably sophisticated research.

What a company's different customers consider value is so complicated that it can be answered only by the customers themselves. Management should not even try to guess at the answers - it should always go to the customer in a systematic quest for them.

Finding out what the customer needs is a very different thing from finding out how satisfied the customer is with your product or service. The second activity is a valid way of improving your aim when you know that you are already hitting the general target area with your product. The first activity is much more fundamental, and is about defining the target you will aim for.

The customers will tell you all you need to know, provided you ask the right questions. The questions for establishing customers' needs are, as you might expect, about the customers and about their needs.

The reason for emphasising this rather obvious point is customers usually believe they are being helpful if they express their needs in terms of the products which they know you already offer. If you encourage them in this, or if you accept it at face value, then you miss the opportunity to learn about what really motivates them. You will also learn very little about needs that lie outside the area of your current provision and which could be the source of new ideas and new products.

Discovering the customers needs is about development, it is not about selling. You are more interested, therefore, in needs not met than in receiving endorsements for your performance.

Every contact and conversation which you have with the customers is an opportunity to learn something new about their needs and their concerns. However, in what follows we shall assume that you are conducting a fairly formal discussion with a customer who knows who you are, and who trusts you. In other situations not all of these conditions will be satisfied and you will have to make some commonsense adjustments.

4.1 PREPARATION

Before you even begin to talk to the customer there are a couple of things you need to clarify in your own mind

1   **What business are you in?** We shall return to this issue later. For the present, it is your way of deciding what is relevant to your discussion, and what ground you will cover.

A doctor, for example, might define their business as

■   dispensing treatments

■   treating illness

■   preventing illness

or

■   creating health

Each successive definition rises above the previous one, and enlarges the focus of the discussion with the patient to include what had previously been part of the context.

Using the first and least definition, the discussion might be confined to how previous treatments had worked and whether it was time for a change. Using the maximum definition of their business, the discussion could legitimately range over the patient's family history, life–style, work habits and career ambitions.

2   Review what you already know about the customer, and about your customers in general. Relevant questions might be

■   how knowledgeable are the customers on the technical aspects of your product?

■   how well are they doing at the moment?

■   what are their business ambitions?

■   what changes are happening in their business and in their industry?

■   how are the changes liable to affect them?

■   what do they value? How do they like to see themselves?

■   whom do they regard as their competitors?

■   how do they define the business they are in?

ACTION POINT 10

Using the ideas in section 4.1

a) Define the business you are in

b) Carry out an analysis of a typical customer

4.2 CONDUCTING THE SESSION

People will tell you everything you could possibly want to know about themselves and their work, and what they like and dislike, and what they find easy and difficult, and much more. All that is needed is that

■   they trust you

■   there is something in it for them

■   you ask the right questions

■   you are a good listener

None of these are difficult to achieve; but they do not come naturally. Most of us have to work on them, and make some conscious effort to keep them under control. Here are some guidelines that will fit most situations, but you will have to adapt them to your own case.

4.3 CREATING TRUST

The biggest single cause of distrust is not knowing the intentions of the other person.

If I do not know why you are questioning me, or what you are trying to achieve by it, I am likely to feel uneasy and at a disadvantage. If your intentions are honourable why shouldn't you tell me what they are? I will be reduced to guessing at your intentions, and will probably go on the defensive.

If you have nothing to hide don't hide it. The following are not meant to be ready–made scripts, but are examples of how it can be done

> 'In our business we need to be sure that we are keeping up to date on our customer's needs; and that is why I would like to take some of your time to talk about you and your business ....'
>
> '.......... We make a lot of assumptions about our customers, and maybe we think that we know more than we really do. That is why we need your help, every now and then, to make sure we really understand what is on our customer's minds'
>
> 'I need some information that only you can provide, and that is ....'

Few people can refuse an open and direct appeal for help. People withhold help only when they feel they are being manipulated. If you have ever been tapped for money in the street you will know that 'I need a pound for a meal' gets better results than 'You've got a generous face , Sir'.

4.4   WHAT'S IN IT FOR THEM?

Being consulted on matters that interest you is, in some measure, its own reward, but you cannot use it as such

> 'I shall be asking you some questions; and what's in it for you is the pleasure of being listened to while you talk about yourself'.

So, you do not need to offer extravagant inducements, but you do need at least to acknowledge the value of your informants time. There are a number of ways in which you might do this

- make it clear that you owe your informant a comparable favour, and they can call it in at any time

- offer them some information of equal value in their business. For example: first sight of a new product; samples of what other people in their kind of business are doing (without betraying confidences); or, simply ask them what they would like to learn from you

Fall back on the basic human motivations: the three things that you can safely assume everybody wants

1   To belong: to be accepted as a member of their group.

2   To be an individual: to be recognised as distinctive from the
        others in some way.

3   To make a difference: to feel that what they do has some impact
        or effect on the world outside themselves.

There has to be a way to use these to help your informant to feel good about
helping you. For example

> 'I am asking you to help in this because your business matches
> exactly the kind of business that we want to cultivate' (belonging).
>
> 'You have used our products in creative ways in the past; and you
> are always very clear on what you want' (individuality).
>
> 'Whatever I learn from you will feed into the development of our
> next generation of products' (impact).

Once you are aware of these basic motivators it is quite easy to make the links
to them. Their effect is to produce a dramatic increase in goodwill. Notice that
it has nothing to do with being insincere, or 'soft soaping' the customer. It is
entirely about giving credit where it is due.

4.5   ASKING THE RIGHT QUESTIONS

Asking the Right Questions 1

All learning begins with a question; because a question expresses a wish to
know something that you do not know already. If we use the word 'leverage'
to describe the power of a question to produce information, then it is clear that
some kinds of questions have much more leverage than others. The first
important distinction is between closed and open questions.

Closed questions are the sort that invite a Yes or No answer, or force a choice
on the respondent. They will typically take the form of 'Is it .... ?' 'Do you ....
?' 'Has it .... ?' Since there are only two possible answers to these questions you
already know that the answer has to be one or the other. You have an even
chance of guessing the answer without even asking the question.

> 'Would you like tea or coffee?' is similarly a closed question
> because it limits the reply to two options.

People may give you a full answer in reply to a closed question; but they are doing it out of the kindness of their hearts, so to speak. because the question itself does not invite it.

> 'Would you like tea or coffee?' 'Well, actually I would like a tequila and bitters with a cherry on top'.

Closed questions have low leverage. You have to work very hard to get any learning from closed questions.

A variation on closed questions, with even less leverage, is the leading question. Leading questions contain an assumption, or strongly prompt the respondent towards the answer that is expected or wanted.

> 'I don't suppose you like Chinese food, do you?'
>
> 'Wasn't that a boring programme?'
>
> 'Most people find our Mark II Widgets very easy to use – how about you?'

If I give the expected answer to all of these questions, what have you learned? Either I do in fact agree with you, or I disagree but I do not want to disappoint your expectation. Since you may never know which of these is the case, you are none the wiser after asking the question than you were before.

Open questions are the sort that begin with an interrogative word like what, why, how, when, who, or their equivalent. Questions of this sort have maximum leverage because they do not set predetermined limits on the answer. They get the respondent to construct their own reply from their own materials.

The secret of successful learning is to use the greatest leverage, and get the maximum return for your questions. Whenever you feel a closed question coming on, pause for a moment and consider whether you might rephrase it to get more value. Once you get into the habit you will find that it actually takes less effort to frame an open question than a closed one.

It is easier to ask

- ■ 'What do you like about the new box files?...' .(Reply 1)
- ■ 'Anything else?' ... (Reply 2) etc

than to ask

■   'Is the price OK?' ... (Reply 1)

■   'Are they strong enough for your use?' ...(Reply 2)

■   'Do they stay shut when they are full, or do they spring open?' ... (Reply 3) etc

In the first case the customer is doing the work, and in the second case you are.

Asking the Right Questions 2 – The Three–Legged Stool

As you know, the three–legged stool or the tripod table will stand firm on any ground. Add a fourth leg and your table starts to rock. The words **what**, **why** and **how** have a similar capacity to keep any discussion in contact with the ground – down to earth you might say. That explains the title of this sub–chapter.

They are fundamental to any piece of training or instruction

'this is what I want you to do'	The **Task**
'this is why you should do it'	The **Objective**
'this is how to do it'	The **Method**

They are similarly fundamental in selling

'this is what you are buying'	The **Product**
'this is why you should buy it'	The **Benefits**
'this is how you can buy it'	**Terms and Price**

And in getting a comprehensive view of your customers needs, they are virtually all you will need, if you can handle them skilfully.

What? will be your usual starting point, to get the basic facts.

Why? enables you to discover the objectives, motives and intentions of your customer; an insight into what drives their decisions.

How? enables you to get into the details of their plans, methods and techniques.

Before we go on to see how this might work in practice – a word of warning about the use of **why** questions.

Why gives you understanding; it takes you inside people's minds; it helps you to learn things you would never learn from observation. However, adults tend to avoid using it because it can sound aggressive, or accusing, or possibly naive

■ 'why did you cancel your order?'

■ 'why did you reorganise your stock department?'

■ 'why did you redesign your shop front?'

All of these blunt questions could invite a defensive reaction. Even though your customer has nothing to hide, and probably has something to gain by being better understood, questions of this kind could remind him that what you are asking is none of your business. For these reasons it is useful to develop a set of plausible alternatives to **why**, which draw out the same information. For example

■ 'what benefits were you looking to get from your new opening hours?

■ 'what considerations led you to redesign your packaging?'

■ 'what was behind your decision to move to a new site?'

All of the phrases underlined are equivalent to **why**, but have a more user–friendly tone.

Asking the Right Questions 3 – Working to a Flexible Plan

Who plans wins. There will be things that you can specify in advance that you want to learn from your interview, and you will want to make sure that all these items are covered. But you do not want to miss making valuable discoveries just because they are not on your predetermined agenda.

A flexible plan is one which allows for discoveries and surprises, and which also sticks to the point. It is as much technique as plan, and it has two vital components

■ a list of key points which you can use as 'stepping stones' in the conversation. Provided you visit each one of them in the course of the conversation it does not matter who raises them or in what order they are considered

■ a clear idea of what is not relevant. You need to be able to recognise when the conversation has crossed the line into irrelevance, and be able to bring it back on track

For example, if you were working for a Contract Cleaning Company, and you were preparing to interview the Office Manager of one of your customers; some of the stepping stones you might definitely want to visit are

■   what does **clean** mean to them? What are their standards? How do they judge them? Does 'clean' include 'tidy'?

■   what feedback do they get from the staff about the cleaning?

■   could they do more of their own cleaning?

■   what are the 'eyesores'?

■   what should be on the schedule: daily, weekly, monthly, annually, ad hoc?

■   earliest times to start, latest time to finish?

■   adequacy of bins etc?

■   what changes are planned in the office layouts and contents?

■   what 'problems' do they have with the cleaning?

■   what do they need that they are not getting?

You do not wish to get side–tracked onto

■   cost, prices, discounts

■   plumbing, drains and the shortcomings of their facilities

■   individual employees (yours or the customer's)

Armed with this plan of what is definitely in and what is definitely out of the conversation, you could manage it in a fairly relaxed way and remain receptive to new ideas and insights. Using open questions, and What, Why, How, you can explore the full range of issues.

Suppose you discover that

■   'if the place smells clean it somehow looks cleaner'

■   tidiness is inseparable from the impression of cleanness in an open plan office. They expect all partitions, chairs and bins to be returned to their proper positions, not just left where they are found

■   they are about to install a networked computer system, and are concerned about pests getting into the cable trunking, and about the dirt traps formed by the 'spaghetti' behind the desks

■   the office staff like the cleaners to arrive before they leave, so that they can give them special instructions

■ disposing of used tea bags and the coffee dregs in disposable cups is a 'nightmare'

■ some staff would like to be sure that their waste paper is recycled

It is very unlikely that you could have come to these conclusions on your own, without actually asking the customer. Equally, it would be surprising if you could not use some of them to add value to your service and to form the basis for a new and more profitable contract with the customer.

4.6 BEING A GOOD LISTENER

Listening, like driving a car and making a good cup of tea, is one of those activities which no–one ever confesses to doing badly, while they cannot think of many others who do it well. This unbalanced view of the world gives us a clue to the underlying problem.

Listening appears to be 'doing what comes naturally', but in fact it is a skill which has to be learned and practised. It is a key skill in dealing with customers and discovering their needs, because if you do it badly you may never know until it is too late.

Frequently we hear only what we want to hear and what we expect to hear, and we come away confirmed in what we already knew. Nothing is changed, nothing is learned. However, listening to learn and to change is a completely different kind of experience.

At the simplest level listening is not interrupting. But even this is not as simple as it sounds. By 'interrupting' we do not just mean stopping the other person from talking, we also mean interrupting with the noise in your head. What you thought they were going to say, your agreement or disagreement, your alternative views, where you have heard it before, who they remind you of: all of these are ways of listening to yourself instead of the other person.

Listening is not natural, it requires an effort of the will and an effort of the intellect in putting yourself into the position of the other person and trying to understand what they are saying in their terms not yours. The skill of listening is to do everything possible to understand the other person. Mainly this means concentrating your attention upon them, looking as well as listening, and taking in all the signals, not just the expected ones. It also means encouraging the other person to tell you more, and making sure that you have understood.

ACTION POINT 11

Use as a model someone who you feel is a good listener. What signals do they give out that convey to you that they are listening and are interested in what you say?

In conversation we give out many subtle signals which tell the other person that we have heard enough and now it's our turn: looking away, raising the eyebrows, opening the mouth, and so on. In response to these the other person will often break off before they have said everything they want to say. Conversely, if you get a grip on your subtle signals, and continue to look the other person in the eye, make encouraging noises, and do not come in when the other person pauses, the other person is likely to carry on talking beyond the point where they intended to stop. It is in this part of the conversation, the part which would not otherwise happen, that most of the learning takes place.

Given time and space, and the expectant listener, people will offer more supporting detail for their views, more reasons for their actions, and suggest solutions to their own problems. The learning, therefore, works both ways, You the listener gain a richer understanding of the other person's world; and, at the same time, the other person creates for themselves a clearer picture of their own goals, motives and options – in other words **what** they want, **why** they want it, and **how** they can get it. This is why, when you are doing your investigations of customers' needs, you will often find that your interviewees react as if you were doing them a favour, instead of vice versa. Good listening makes the favour mutual.

How do you know that you have really understood what the other person is saying, and you are not just fitting them into your preconceived mould?

■ You ask questions to clarify, and to check that you have heard and understood

'Have I got it right? You are saying that ....'

'Let me confirm. You have told me that .... Is that it?'

'Could you tell me again what the problem was with .... '

■ You summarise, at natural break points

'We have talked about quality standards, and you have said ....
Is there anything I have missed out?'

'As I hear it, there are four main areas for improvement. They are
.... Does that cover the points you raised?'

Again people will be gratified to receive this kind of feedback which confirms that their efforts to communicate have not been in vain.

CHAPTER SUMMARY

Having completed this chapter you should now

■ see the importance of finding out your customer's needs

■ understand the need to create trust in your customer

■ know the various questions you can use to find out your customer's needs

■ be aware of the need to be a good listener

If you are unsure about any of these areas, go back and re-read the relevant part(s) of the text.

5 DESIGNING YOUR PRODUCT FROM THE CUSTOMER'S NEEDS

We have seen that customers do not need things; they need the services, benefits or advantages which the things can provide. Once you stop thinking of your products as things, but as a means of satisfying the various needs of the customers, then you begin to see that you and the customers both have choices. The customers can chose to use you or your competitors. They can often choose to satisfy their needs by alternative means which by–pass you and your competitors. For your part, you can choose how far you wish to go in meeting their needs.

The diagram below illustrates the point. It shows how a customer's high–level and abstract need can be resolved into a series of increasingly specific needs. These specific needs can be satisfied, more or less, by a number of different products and services. Particular businesses may chose to offer various combinations of these products and services. Some combinations seem to fit together better than others, and form a coherent whole, but there is still scope for offering imaginative combinations which break the familiar mould of clothes shops, dry cleaners, and so on.

What the customer wants	Matching products and services
Smart, distinctive appearance	'Personal Image' Consultancy
Individual appearance	Made to measure/designer clothes
Choice of wardrobe	Off the peg/extensive stock/clothes hire/express cleaning
Clothes that last	Quality materials/gentle cleaning/re-texturing
Clothes that look tidy	Crease-resistant material/repair service/cleaning and pressing
Clothes that look clean	Laundry/dry cleaning/laundrette/domestic washing machine

The decision which you make on how far you will go to satisfy your customer is one important part of the decision of what business you are in.

5.1   WHAT BUSINESS ARE YOU IN?

There are three interdependent aspects of your business that you need to consider before you can answer this question

■   what are you good at?

■   what general area of customer needs are you satisfying?

■   how are you different from other suppliers?

Some companies define their business in terms of only one of the variables. This may be simple and memorable, but it is a rather unbalanced way of looking at yourself. We shall look at all three variables in turn and then examine how they hang together.

What are you good at?

This question is sometimes posed as 'What are your **core competencies**?' The idea is that every organisation has, or ought to have, some peculiar strengths which are expressed in their current product range but which are not identical with that range. Identifying your core competencies gives you a clue to what else you might be doing that would exploit the strengths you now have. Alternatively it could alert you to the fact that you are not keeping up with the times.

For example

> The 3M company has defined its core competence as 'putting coatings on thin materials' (or words to that effect). It is this common factor which unites the strange variety of thing which they produce. These range from sandpaper, to sticky tape, to photographic film, to recording tape, to floppy discs. The peculiar nature of their core competence means that they are not tied exclusively to any particular type of customer. It also means that they have to be innovative, and bring out a continuous flow of new products, because most of their products will be low–tech and relatively easy to copy.

Now let me ask you a question. Take a company like Canon. You all know this company. What businesses do you know today that Canon is in? You answer cameras for sure, copiers, fax machines, printers, sophisticated equipment for semi-conductor production. How did you interpret the word 'businesses'? You interpret it as 'products'. Now if you ask Canon what business they are in, they would give you a very different story.

They would say that they were in

- Precision mechanics
- Fine optics
- Micro electronics

Their answer is in terms of underlying core competencies.

I would argue that, in the medium to long term, the battle for global leadership is a battle for leadership in core competence areas, and it takes much longer to build a core competence, probably ten to twenty years, than it does simply to launch a particular product.

What General Area of Customer Needs are You Satisfying?

This is a question about how you want to appear to the customer. When the customer sees your name, or thinks about you, what set of needs should they associate with you? How inclusive do you want it to be?

The value of asking this question is that it enables you to compare your own ambitions, and your own view of what your business provides, with the customer's expectations and image of your business. If the two are not completely aligned than you have some work to do.

For example

If you were in the transport business, these are some of the choices you might have to make

Size of load

- no load too small?
- no load too large?

Range

- local?
- national?
- international?
- worldwide?

Speed

- same day?
- 48 hours?
- by arrangement

Frequency

- scheduled runs?
- on demand?
- both?

Collection/delivery

- depot to depot?
- door to door?

Other services

- courier?
- security handling?
- house removals?
- packing?
- customs documentation?
- vehicle leasing

Each of these decisions enlarges or restricts your coverage, and to that extent draws in or excludes particular kinds of customers and needs. Whatever decision you come to, you need to offer a usable combination of services to the customer, and to present a clear image to them. To use your services intelligently, and to make it a regular habit, they need to know what to expect.

ACTION POINT 12

Whom are you pleasing?

Consider your own organisation or section.

1   List the services which you have on offer for the customer

2   Which ones are most used, least used, not used at all?

3   Do your customers expect you to do anything not on the list?

4   Why do you think they expect that?

5   Could you do it if you wanted to?

6   Would it be worthwhile?

How Different are You?

If there is any sort of competition in your business then there must be some way in which the customers can tell the difference between you and the others.

If there is no difference at all between what you and your competitors produce, then your product is a **commodity** and you are not really in competition at all.

A commodity is, by definition, an undifferentiated product. Any item is identical to any other. Agricultural products and raw materials are the classic commodities. They are traded in specialised commodity markets or exchanges. The individual producer has no control over the price, he only has the choice of whether to sell or not. Malting barley, Brent crude, copper bars, herrings, are all traded in a similar way. The products are classified according to an objective and well-understood system. Price is the only consideration which influences the buyer.

At the other extreme of differentiation you have the unique work of art, or the completely customised item: an architect-designed house, for example. It is almost as if a separate market were created for each of these individual items. There is no direct competition. There are just other ways in which the customers might spend their money.

Somewhere along the scale between these extremes lies most of the products that you are likely to be concerned with.

Companies producing simple and basic products live constantly in fear of commoditisation. This is the situation where the customers make no distinction between their product and those of the competitors, and the only way they can make their product more attractive is by cutting the price. Hotel rooms in holiday resorts are virtually in this category. They are traded among tour operators like barrels of oil. The consumers are buying a package which bears the tour operator's name; the hotel is just one component of the package with no particular identity of its own.

The makers of other simple food or consumer products, like instant coffee, baked beans, washing powder or plant fertilisers defend themselves against commoditisation by making the most of what little difference there is. This accounts for the amount of money spent on advertising, to etch their brand names on our minds; and the fancy packaging, designed to be instantly recognisable; and the constant small changes, new smells, new sizes, new additives, designed to present the product as evolving and developing, but still keeping its original identity.

At the other end of the scale, where the product is essentially customised, many producers are busy developing standardised components and modular units so that they do not have to design each new product from scratch. Double glazing would be a simple example of this. Most building and construction work would provide more complex examples of this approach.

A more typical approach to differentiation is to offer various kinds of personal help to the customer before and after their decision to buy: making a 'service sandwich'.

Before the decision you can offer

■   advice

■   demonstrations

■   information

■   education

After the decision you can offer

■   installation

■   technical support

■   help–lines

■   repair and replacement

■   upgrades

■   privileged access to new products

Any one can make their product different from the rest. Rice, which the grocer used to scoop out of a sack into a brown paper bag, can be put through some minimal process so that the grains do not stick together when they are boiled. It can then be branded and packaged and sold at a huge premium. And customers will refuse to buy ordinary rice if Uncle Ben's is out of stock.

Water, which used to come out of the domestic tap, can be named and labelled to give it an aura of country simplicity, zest for life, or continental chic. People will ask for it by name in the pub, and pay good money to have their self–image reinforced.

If they can do it so can you.

ACTION POINT 13

Look at your product through your customers' eyes

■ what makes it different from what your competitors are offering?

■ which of the differences represent added value as far as the customer is concerned?

5.2   HOW VARIABLE ARE YOUR CUSTOMERS?

So far we have been discussing the customer or customers as if they were either one person or a group with identical needs. It is a convenient manner of speaking but it has its limitations.

Obviously your customers are all different in ways that matter a lot to them. The question that we need to ask is, are they different in ways that ought to matter to you?

Do they fall into any identifiable groups or categories, whose needs are different enough to warrant different provision or different treatment from you.

Some possible significant differences are

■   spending power – value of their custom

■   technical knowledge and expertise

■   clarity of their requirement

■   type of use

We shall look at each of these in turn and consider how you might respond.

5.3   SPENDING POWER OF THE CUSTOMER

The value of a particular transaction or sale may not be a reasonable measure of the value of a customer. If a customer is someone who gives their custom to you on a regular and recurring basis, then their value as a customer should be estimated over the lifetime of the relationship.

If you are a car dealer, and your customer is spending £12,000 on a car you may feel pleased with your day's work. But suppose they renew their car every three years; over the course of a working life of, say, 30 years they will buy 10 cars. The total value of these will be £120,000 at present values, possibly more if their work prospers and they go up–market. If you add in the possibility that they may influence a couple of colleagues to give you their custom, you could be looking at more than a £1/4 million. At that rate it is worth putting some resources into securing their loyalty so that they will want to come back next time.

Many companies find ways of identifying their high value customers and giving them privileges, which recognise their value to the company and give them a reason for continuing to give it their custom.

The 'Frequent Flyer' clubs which airlines form, under various names, for their regular passengers; the American Express Gold Card and Platinum Card, are typical examples of ways in which big spenders are singled out for a higher level of service, without downgrading the normal level of service given to the rest.

In accounting terms you could say it is the equivalent of giving a discount for a bulk purchase; but in human terms it has much more impact, because it personalises the privilege.

5.4   TECHNICAL EXPERTISE OF THE CUSTOMER

Consider the technical expertise of the customer in the following examples.

Supplying studio lighting to the BBC, and supplying shop lighting to a fashion store.

Selling musical instruments to beginners, and selling to professional musicians.

Designing central heating systems for a domestic user, and designing a heating system for an architect's office.

In each case the hard, tangible product which is changing hands may be very much the same, but clearly the nature of the transaction is very different. The difference lies in the relative authority of the supplier and the customer, what each one expects of the other, and the way in which the buying decision is made.

In general expert customers expect at least a comparable level of expertise from their opposite numbers in the supplying companies because they want to solve problems. The inexpert customers also expect a reasonable level of expertise; but this time it is to help them make a sensible choice and advise them on the proper use of their new purchase. This diagram summarises the outcome of all the possible combinations of high and low expertise in customers and supplier.

What is clear from this diagram is that there is no advantage to be got from low expertise on the part of the supplier. This sounds obvious, but it is very often disregarded in those companies who put the first (and possibly the last!) contact with the customer into the hands of their least experienced staff.

I occasionally try my hand at DIY. I have no particular skills or expertise, and I have no interest in block–board, screws, brackets, drills and plugs, as such. I am interested in, say, a secure and level shelf, strong enough to support a hi–fi system.

I take my requirements along to the local hardware shop, and the proprietor and I talk about my walls and what they are made of. We talk about the size and weight of the equipment which I want to shelve.

I come away with a set of parts which I know will serve their purpose. I also come away with some useful tips which make me feel confident that I can do the job.

I have paid considerably more for my set of things, than I would have paid at the local 'Superstore'; where I would also have had more choice. But I feel I have made a good bargain. I did not want things, I wanted a solution to my problem.

5.5   CLARITY OF CUSTOMERS' NEEDS

This may often be related to the customer's level of technical expertise, but it is a separate issue.

As a supplier you can satisfy a need only when it has come down to what we might call your **operating level**. For example, suppose you were running a restaurant and a customer came in and said she wanted 'a meal'. If you were offering a single set dinner, then her request would be sufficient for you to meet her needs. However, if you were offering only à–la–Carte meals, her request would amount to asking to see the menu, rather than to ordering a meal. You could not set your production machine in motion until you had more specific information on her requirements for first course, main course, vegetables, and so on.

The amount of detail you need, your operating level, depends therefore on the range of choices that you offer. When a customer first comes to you they may be anywhere, from having a notion that you might help them, to knowing precisely what they want. The further 'upstream' they are, the more help, advice, information and counsel they will need.

The personal computer business is typical of businesses where some customers will have done their homework and have a very precise shopping list of hardware and software. Others, meanwhile, will have only a vague notion that a computer might help them to sort out the problems they have in managing their accounts, or controlling their correspondence and producing decent–looking reports.

Does anyone cater for this second type of customer?

It is quite likely that they will never even pluck up the courage to go into the shop, for fear of having their ignorance exposed. Computer salespeople are notorious for being more interested in computers than in people. As a result they rarely get to see the customer who does not already have a good idea of what they want. For lack of suitable provision they remain a **potential** customer who never converts into an **actual**.

If you are dealing mainly with business customers, professionals and people in the trade, this issue of how you accommodate the vague or inexpert customer may not apply. But the general issue of user–friendliness remains. Do you make it easy to do business with you? Do the customers have to understand how your organisation works before they can get things done? Are there any potential customers out there who never make contact, because they feel ill–prepared to deal with you?

Type of Use

This is probably the most obvious source of variety in customers. It is obvious because it is the factor which is most likely to be already accounted for in your products. You probably already classify your products into categories like

- domestic, commercial, industrial
- light–duty, heavy–duty
- continuous use, intermittent use
- single user, many users

These represent product groups, or product lines, but do they also represent types of customers? If they do not, then it has some implications for the way in which you organise your customer contact.

If your business is organised by product line, but your customers are not, then you could be making them run around unnecessarily. If they have to make contact with a variety of different people because they have a variety of different needs, then you are giving the customer a problem which ought to be yours to solve.

'One–stop shopping' is the customer's ideal. If you fall short of that ideal then you have some scope for improving your service.

How Can You Add Value to Your Product?

The general rule for adding value to your product is very simple

Meet more of your customer's needs

What this means in practice is that you need to have a full and detailed understanding of your customers' needs, and you need to see the relationship between the customer and your company as a continuous whole. With these perspectives you will be able to see opportunities for expanding your coverage in two dimensions, which we might call **breadth** and **depth**.

Breadth means extending your service upstream and downstream of the actual purchase contract. Depth means extending the range of needs that you are prepared to satisfy.

Most of the ideas on how you might do this have come out already. What follows, then, is a checklist of these ideas, which relates them to the various stages of a transaction.

Access
- are you easy to contact?
- does each customer relate to a single individual who takes overall responsibility for their interests?
- do customers have to learn your procedures and understand your organisation structure in order to get what they want?

Establishing Need
- are you asking open questions?
- are you helping the customer to express their objectives, in terms of the performance and benefits which they expect?

Clarifying Needs
- are you prompting the customer to take into account the interests of other users?
- are you matching your technical information and problem-solving to the customer's level of expertise?
- are you giving the customer all the information they need to make an informed and intelligent choice?

Deciding the Provision
- do you offer one-stop shopping?
- are you prepared to acquire for the customer things which you do not normally make or provide?

Follow-up

- do you offer post-delivery service: Installation; Commissioning; User Training?

- do you offer continuing support: Hotlines; information updates; follow-up calls; checks on customer's satisfaction?

- do you leave the customer with the impression that you expect to do further business with them?

ACTION POINT 14

Using those questions in the checklist above which are relevant to your own situation assess the breadth and depth of the service you offer to your customers.

CHAPTER SUMMARY

Having completed this chapter you should now

■   know what your core competencies are

■   be aware of the type of customer needs you satisfy

■   understand what is meant by 'commodity'

■   see the importance of customer spending power

■   understand how to add value to your product

If you are unsure about any of these areas, go back and re-read the relevant part(s) of the text.

6 DEVELOPING NEW PRODUCTS

The development of new products is a routine part of staying in business. Products die, or lose their popularity, or become technically obsolete, or are surpassed by new competitive products. This is as much a part of the natural cycle of products as the birth, maturity and death of living things. As a general rule, if you have a product which continues unchanged for a long period it is likely to be close to the commodity end of the differentiation scale. Products which are highly differentiated are most likely to need continual development or replacement.

For these reasons the development of new products cannot be left to chance. It is not a mysterious process. It does not have to rely upon exceptional creativity or the elusive 'breakthrough'. Any company can do it, if it has appropriate policies and systems.

In the rest of this chapter we shall look, firstly at the range of policies which might drive the search for new products, and secondly at the possible source of ideas for new products.

6.1 POLICIES AND GUIDELINES

If the search for new products is not to be a random or accidental event it needs to be underpinned by some policies or guidelines, which all staff can understand. The purpose of these policies is to focus the attention of the staff on where the need for new products will show itself.

Examples of such policies might be.

Build on Competitive Strengths

If you already have an established superiority in some area of your product or service, it is the likeliest source of continued advantage in the future. But you have to maintain it and enhance it; there is no such thing as 'effortless superiority' in business. You therefore need to know what your strengths are; but, even more, you need to know which strengths are important to the customer. These are your competitive strengths, the ones that give you an advantage in your market. The other strengths only make you feel good.

Keep a Hold on Existing Customers

Do whatever is needful to retain the individuals who are your existing customers. Be prepared to change as they change. Are they going up market? Are they getting more adventurous? Are they becoming more fashion–conscious? Are they more concerned about conserving natural resources? Are they worrying about getting old? So are you.

How can you develop your product so that it keeps pace with these changes in the tastes and habits of the customers? How can you identify which of these changes require a response from you, and which you can disregard.

Find New Customers for Existing Products

Are there any identifiable groups of people who could be customers but are not buying? What gets in the way of their buying? What can you do to remove the barrier?

Usually the barrier is about the image and the associations which have become attached to the product, rather than any external characteristic of the product itself.

Getting adults to use Johnson's 'Baby' products is an example of this policy in action. Another example is Lucozade, which used to be associated with recovery from illness, and is now presented as an 'energy' drink for athletes.

Exploit Developments in Technology

Identify those areas where current technology is a limiting factor in the performance of your product. Monitor developments in technology and seize the opportunities as they arise.

For example, if you are making equipment for anglers, the design of your rods always involves a trade–off among spring, strength and weight.

Similarly your fishing lines are the best compromise that you can make among strength, flexibility and thinness. In each case the optimum solution is limited by the characteristics of the materials currently available. New materials could change the performance of your equipment very significantly; but you will probably have to wait until someone else develops them.

Attain a Target Share of the Market

This policy focuses on your position in relationship to your competitors.

Your target might be to dominate the market; in which case you will be constantly seeking to develop advantages which you competitors cannot match.

If your aim is to lead the market you will be continuously looking for ways to stay ahead or outperform the other. They may follow, but you will get there first.

If your aim is to maintain your position in, say, the top five producers, or to remain in contention with the leader, then you will be constantly monitoring your competitors' activities, finding out what you can do about their plans and intentions, and anticipating how they might respond to your initiatives.

Whatever your particular target may be, if it is defined in terms of you market position then it involves you in the strategic game of anticipating and reacting to the competition who are anticipating and reacting to you. The game does not usually have a conclusion. It goes on for ever.

ACTION POINT 15

Think of one particular product or service that you offer your customers.

1. Identify your company's competitive strengths.

2. How does your company ensure that existing customers are kept satisfied?

3. Can you identify new groups of potential customers and suggest ways to win their custom?

4. Can technological development enhance this product or service in a new way?

5. What is the aim of your company with regard to the market share of this product or service?

6.2 SOURCES OF IDEAS FOR NEW PRODUCTS

For present purposes we shall treat new products and improvements to existing products as being essentially the same thing. In practice the distinction between 'new' and 'improved' is more a matter of how the change is presented to the customer than of what sort of change it is.

We have already seen that for most companies the development of new products is not an optional extra activity but an essential part of their survival kit. Therefore they cannot afford to leave it to chance or to inspiration; they have to cultivate it systematically. They have to identify the people who are likely to have ideas for new products, and then tap into these sources and make sure that the ideas are collected and evaluated. For most companies the main sources of ideas will be

- customers
- competitors
- staff
- research and development

Customers

Your customers are the final arbiters on whether a product change is an improvement or not. For that reason they are the most important source of ideas for product development. You can use formal or informal methods for gathering these ideas.

Informally they are informing you every day of their needs, their complaints, their reactions to your existing products and services, what they like and dislike, their aims and their dearest wishes. If you have the wit to see them as such, all of these equate to suggestions on how you might develop your products.

The problem for you is that the information is given piecemeal: by word of mouth to all your customer–contact staff, by letter of complaint or commendation, by report cards. All of these need somehow to be captured, brought together and examined to see what patterns are hidden in the information.

More formally you can organise market research to poll your customers reactions and suggestions.

You can assemble Consultative Groups, User Groups, Focus Groups, whatever you wish to call them, and get them to advise you on developments which they would like to see, and which they would be willing to buy. It is in their own interest to exert their influence on you, so your customers will usually be quite willing to be used by you in this way.

Competitors

Your competitors are probably as smart as you, perhaps smarter in some ways. If they are the leaders then there must be some reason for their current superiority. If you are leading them, they probably feel that they must 'try harder'. Either way, you should not be too proud to learn from them.

It is rarely necessary to resort to espionage or undercover operations to check out what your competitors are doing. Virtually anything you may wish to know about them is legitimately and freely available to you and anyone else

- product advertisements
- recruitment advertisements
- promotional materials
- report and accounts
- reports in the trade press and national press
- direct observation and personal experience of your own staff and customers
- examples of their products

All of these are available to anyone, and the sum total of them amounts to a very rich picture of their strengths and weaknesses, their objectives and plans. You may not in the end be able to do very much with this information. But not having it could be very costly, if your competitors are able to take you by surprise with new developments which you could have anticipated, if you had taken the trouble to read the signs.

Your own staff

Everyone knows that the staff who have hands on the product – manufacturing, assembling or installing – and the staff who have face–to–face contact with the customer, are potentially the most fruitful source of ideas for improving the product and for improving the efficiency of your operation. However, most companies do not have the systems necessary to encourage the growth of ideas in the first place, and to progress them through to plans and actions.

Most ideas are suppressed before they are formed, because the employee does not know who to tell them to. If the idea survives this first hurdle and does find expression it is probably not listened to. If it is listened to it is probably not acted upon.

There will always be a high natural wastage rate in ideas, because a lot of them will be not very new, or not very practical. It is folly to add an unnatural wastage to an already high natural one, by maintaining barriers to the free flow of ideas.

You need an abundance of ideas to be produced if a reasonable number of them are to be finally adopted as product improvements, having survived all the natural hazards of evaluation for relevance, feasibility, practicality, and cost effectiveness. You need more than just a suggestion box.

Companies that have successfully tapped into this source of ideas have concentrated on removing the internal barriers and unblocking the flow. Here is a checklist that suggests some ways of doing this

- record all suggestions and ideas
- keep the documentation simple
- encourage tentative and half–baked ideas; do not expect an elaborate business proposal
- allow provision for staff who are put off by form–filling to offer their suggestions by word of mouth
- assign clear responsibility for reviewing and progressing ideas
- review all ideas quickly and give feedback to all the originators
- look for some merit and potential value in every suggestion, even those which will not be implemented in their original form
- reward all good suggestions, not only those which are going to be implemented
- give the originator of a successful suggestion a role in implementing it

Research and Development

The management of Research and Development is a specialised discipline in its own right, and we do not wish to venture very far into it here. On the face of it, a specialist unit, devoted solely to discovery and innovation, looks like it could be the answer to all the company's needs for product development. However, it could also be a trap for the unwary. At the risk of being very unfair to R and D, we shall offer here a few words of caution. The R and D department

- ■ can easily become the only legitimate source of ideas and innovation. It takes away the pressure from other departments to take responsibility for their own developments

- ■ can become the internal customer for all ideas and suggestions. In this role it is more likely to act as a brake than an accelerator in getting the ideas evaluated and implemented

- ■ is typically protected from direct contact with the external customers. But it is these customers who are the proper arbiters of whether an idea is a good one or not. Whoever makes those judgements should be able to speak with the authority of the external customer

- ■ is not responsible for the implementation of product improvements and innovations. It therefore tends to measure its output in terms of discoveries, reports and recommendations, rather than in terms of 'real' product development

None of these problems is insuperable, but the solution often requires changing the habits of a lifetime. That is why in many companies the R and D department carries on R and D'ing, while the real product development takes place somewhere else.

ACTION POINT 16

Think about the most recent product or service introduced by your company. Analyse the sources of the ideas.

CHAPTER SUMMARY

Having completed this chapter you should now

- ■ understand the need for clearly laid down policies regarding new products

- ■ be aware of the policies used in this area

- ■ know what sources there are for new products

- ■ be aware of some of the pitfalls associated with R and D

If you are unsure about any of these areas, go back and re-read the relevant parts of the text.

7 CONSTRAINTS ON SERVICE

Clearly you cannot give all your customers everything they would like all the time. Your resources are not unlimited; and as soon as you start to deal with limited resources you come up against the hard facts of economics.

7.1 WANTS AND EXPECTATIONS

Everything has a cost and as a general rule if you want more of something you have to pay more for it.

How much more you are willing to pay depends on how much you **value** the additional product or service.

That is the complete theory of economics in two sentences. In theory, then, there is a conflict between buyers and sellers; each party wanting to get more and give less, at the other's expense.

When we stop talking of **buyers** and **sellers** and start talking of **businesses** and **customers**, we move beyond the primitive economic theory, towards ways of managing the conflict of interests so that there are no losers. Not being able to give the customers everything they want is not really a problem. You have problems only if you disappoint their **expectations**.

There is not much you can do about what they want; you need to know about it, but it is essentially beyond your control. Their expectations, however, are very much within your control. They are largely created by you; or they are the outcome of some kind of discussion, understanding and agreement between you and the customer.

When we talk about 'constraints on service' we are dealing with the hard facts of size, skills, technology, materials and costs, which set the limits on the products and service you can deliver. Your job is to manage the customer's expectations so that they do not expect more than you are able to deliver. As a general rule, customers are satisfied if their expectations are met or exceeded, and dissatisfied if their expectations are not met. So, whether your performance satisfies or dissatisfies the customer depends not on the nature of the performance but on where it stands in relation to the expectations which you set up.

For example: if you promise a 24 hour delivery and you deliver in 20 hours you will have a satisfied customer. They have their goods four hours earlier than expected. If you promise a 12 hour delivery and you deliver in 13 hours you will have a dissatisfied customer who has had to wait an hour. Measured in hours, the second performance is better than the first. Measured alongside customer expectations the second performance is a disappointment and the first is a winner.

Over committing themselves, and underselling themselves are the two traps that await the supplier who is not clear in their own minds what they can and cannot do. Either way they fail to manage their customers' expectations.

Over–committing is the result of allowing expectations to drift beyond your capacity to perform. 'Try' is the word that gives this game away.

> 'I'll **try** to redo it by the end of the week.'

> 'I'll **try** to expedite the order.'

What the sensible customer ought to say in reply to this kind of statement is 'Will you or won't you? I would rather know now than be disappointed later.' What happens more often is that the customer simply hears it as a promise.

Underselling, on the other hand, is apologising in advance for what you cannot do, and therefore presenting what you can do as a ready–made disappointment.

'I am afraid we can offer only red, blue, yellow and grey.' (You have a choice of four colours.)

'There is no–one on duty after 6 o'clock.' (You can leave a message on the machine at any time.)

'You will have to wait until next Thursday.' (We can turn that round in 5 working days.)

'Our guarantee does not cover misuse by unauthorised personnel.' (If you look after it properly it should last a lifetime.)

Satisfying your customers entails knowing your own constraints and being clear about them, so that the customer's expectations fall within the bounds of what you can deliver. The major sources of these constraints will be

- size
- skills
- state of the Art
- costs

We shall take a brief look at each of these in turn.

7.2 SIZE

Large and small are very imprecise terms. In a business context they can only be understood relative to the total size of the market being served and the size of other companies in the same business. In practice we take these factors into account without thinking, so that we usually have no problem in categorising businesses as large or small.

There are strengths and weaknesses on both sides. The tables below give a summary of what these are – in general; not all of them will apply in all cases.

Small Company	
Typical strengths	**Typical weaknesses**
Personal touch	Labour intensive
Flexible customer service	Limited choice
Fast decisions	Limited capacity
Easy to communicate with	
Skilled staff - generalists	
Low fixed costs	

Large Company	
Typical Strengths	**Typical Weaknesses**
Specialised equipment	Bureaucratic procedures
Large range of services/products	Impersonal
Specialist staff	High fixed cost
	May only handle large jobs

To appreciate how these factors work in different ways in different businesses consider the business of car servicing and printing.

In car servicing the large and small companies are offering essentially the same service. What differentiates them is that the large companies usually specialise in one make of car.

They have specialised diagnostic equipment and stock a comprehensive set of spare parts.

They are frequently organised into departments with fully–trained technicians in supervisory roles, and specialised, semi skilled staff doing the actual work.

The customer deals directly with the reception staff, they rarely see the workshop itself.

Work is done according to standard procedures.

Work schedules are prepared as far in advance as possible.

Customers have to book their service at least a week in advance.

The companies charge premium prices.

By contrast, small companies will usually take on any make of car.

They use general purpose equipment. They do not carry their own range of spares.

Their staff are all generalists.

The customer deals directly with the people who will do the work.

They are often prepared to improvise on methods and schedules, and to carry out work at short notice.

They charge normal, competitive rates.

Customers of the large companies put their confidence in the good name and reputation of the company itself. Customers of the small companies base their judgement on personal recommendations, the impressions they gain of the individuals and the general appearance and atmosphere of the workshop.

In the printing business the consequences of difference in size are quite different from those in the car servicing business. In this case the large companies are capital–intensive, with expensive and powerful equipment. Their fixed costs are very high. They are therefore geared–up to high speed, high volume work, which they can turn over very quickly. The small companies have lower speed, lower capacity equipment and are therefore geared–up to take smaller jobs with a longer turnover time.

What distinguishes the larger and the smaller printing companies is the type of work they take on; from letter heads, business cards, invitations and menus at one end, to large circulations newspapers and magazines at the other, with books, brochures and company reports in the middle. The small companies are physically unable to do the kind of work which the large companies take on, and vice versa.

ACTION POINT 17

Using the information above, make a list of the advantages and disadvantages of the size of the company you work for.

7.3 SKILLS

The particular mix of skills available within the company sets an obvious limit on the service which it can offer the customer, at least in the short run. The range of skills on offer will frequently be related to the size of the company, but the relationship is not a straightforward one. More is not necessarily better. What matters to the customer is that your company's range of skills should form a coherent set, which may be broad or narrow depending on what makes sense in the circumstances.

For example it makes sense to have a business which specialises in unblocking drains because a blocked drain is a self–contained problem for the customer. It would not make sense, however, to have a business which specialised in installing baths and basins but did not plumb them in to the water and drainage; even though the plumbing requires a different set of skills from those needed to position and secure the equipment.

Similarly it makes sense for a company to specialise in replacing car exhausts, because a damaged exhaust presents itself as a discrete problem needing a discrete and urgent solution. On the other hand you could not offer gasket replacement, or wheel alignment, as separate services to the customer. They make sense to the customer only in the context of a more comprehensive maintenance and repair service.

Companies whose specialised skills do not quite correspond with a coherent set of customer needs frequently find that they have to act as brokers, and bring in other 'associates' to enable them to offer a service which feels like a reasonable whole. Building firms of all sizes typically operate in this way.

The customers' views on what constitutes a sensible, self–contained service are liable to change over a period of time; and it is this change which pushes companies to evolve either in the direction of greater specialisation or in the direction of offering a more comprehensive set of services.

While some companies have become specialists in watering the plants in offices, the large accounting firms, for example have evolved into complex organisations offering a wide range of consulting services.

In the case of the accounting firms this is because their customers have come to see the management of money as a vital element of the company's strategy, and not simply as a matter of keeping the accounts and balancing the books. Following the logic of their customers the accounting firms have now gone into consulting work on corporate strategy, mergers and acquisitions, information technology, and even management training.

7.4   STATE OF THE ART

Because this topic is so large we shall be very brief, and simply highlight some of the key points. The development of technology clearly has a continuing and pervasive influence on every aspect of the way in which we design, make and distribute our products and services. But if we consider only the impact which it has on the service which we are able to offer the customer, it can be summarised into four main areas.

1   **Customers' Expectations** – Can you keep up?

Perfectly serviceable goods can be made obsolete if the customer now **expects** a more technically advanced version. To some extent companies are obliged to build the latest technology into their products simply because it exists. This especially true for products which are already high–tech.

If you are engaged in repair and maintenance you will need to be able to repair and maintain whatever the customers are now buying. For example, an increasing proportion of cars are now diesel powered or have electronic ignition systems. Their owners expect the garage service engineer to take these changes in his stride.

2   **Helping Big Companies to Act Small**

Information technology and computerised systems can be used to enable big companies to offer the kind of personalised service which was previously available only from small companies

■   very large distributors can advise you over the phone of what is in stock, and can tell you exactly when your order was assembled and dispatched

■   airlines can keep a record of the seat preferences and travel history of every frequent flyer so that as soon as they give their name to the reservation agent they can be treated as a known customer

■   cars made by mass–production methods can be assembled to the individual customer's specifications of colour, upholstery, engine and extras

3   **Helping Small Companies to Act Big**

Information technology and computer power can also be used to enable small companies to work to a standard and speed that was previously available only from companies able to invest in very expensive and specialised equipment or premises

- any company with a good Desktop Publishing programme can produce high quality ready–to–print copy and illustrations at a cost which makes a very short print run economical

- Computer Aided Design can make one person more productive than a whole drawing office or normal draughtsperson

- the mobile phone, the portable fax, electronic mail and the remote controlled answering machine can make a person accessible at any time in any place. In principle at least, small businesses can be completely dispersed while appearing to the outside world to be constantly available at some notional head office

4   New Solutions to Old Problems

Some problems appear to be insoluble, except at the cost of creating even larger problems elsewhere. They await the arrival of a suitable technology. Until then they have to be accepted as a fact of life.

Cash machines at banks, which now do a lot more than simply dispense cash, finally solved the problem of customers with quick transactions having to wait behind customers with long and complex transactions. As an added bonus, they also gave customers access to their own money outside the bank's restricted opening hours.

Such machines had been 'visualised' for decades at countless brainstorming sessions, but they could not become a reality until the technology existed to verify cards, and count bank notes automatically, and record the transactions.

Power tools have always required a physical connection to a power supply. If you wished to use power tools in remote or awkward places you had to take your generator or your compressor with you. Cordless power tools for serious work had to wait upon the development of rechargeable batteries which could deliver the necessary power at a reasonably portable weight.

In both these cases the new technology was developed by third parties for other uses, but was recognised and taken up by the banks and the power tool companies because it helped them to break free of their existing limitations.

7.5 COSTS

If your company is carrying higher cost than its competitors then you have a problem – unless the extra costs produce some additional value which the customer is prepared to pay for. The good news is that customers are prepared to pay extra for what they perceive to be additional value. The whole of economic theory is founded on this simple principle.

If customers are not willing to pay extra for an 'improved' level of service they are telling you that it does not represent any additional value to them. 'Improved' is your word not theirs; for them it is just 'different'.

Companies which are monopolies, or which are in some way protected from competition, may feel free to pass on higher costs to the consumer in the form of higher prices. But even they cannot force the customer to buy, and price increases which are not matched by value increases will result in reduced business.

The successful company needs to achieve a reasonable and stable balance between costs, value to customer, and price. It will be constantly asking itself these questions

■ where do we have relatively high costs?

■ what value for the customer results from our high costs activities?

■ how are the costs recouped?

■ which customers benefit?

■ can the service or product be differentiated so that those who get the additional value pay for it?

■ if the extra cost produces no benefit, how can we get rid of it?

Here are some examples of how this sort of cost/value audit might work.

You are a menswear retailer. Your costs for premises and stock are higher than your competitors because you keep a comprehensive range of sizes, colours and materials in trousers and jackets.

The value that this represents for the customer is that he has a higher probability of finding exactly what he wants, instead of settling for second best or having to shop around.

Every customer benefits from this, but especially the hard to fit and the hard to please. You may conclude from this that you are attracting customers who are

CHAPTER SUMMARY

Having completed this chapter you should now

■ Know what is meant by over-committing and underselling to your customers

■ understand what constraints exist in a company's capacity to deliver a product

■ be aware of the impact of technology on the design, production and distribution of products and services

■ see the need to view 'additional value' of a product or service from the customer's point of view

■ know how additional costs may be turned to your advantage

If you are unsure about any of these areas, go back and re-read the relevant part(s) of the text.

8 SEGMENTATION AND PRICING

Segmentation is the process of identifying groups among your customers and tailoring your products so that you are making a separate provision for each 'market segment'. The aim of segmentation is to protect the business and to exploit the full potential of the market at the same time.

Examples of segmentation might be

■ in the travel trade – business travellers, holiday–makers, other. The segment called 'other' could itself be broken down into further segments such as 'visiting relatives', immigrants, pilgrims, educational, and so on.

Each of these segments is based upon the passenger's reason for travel. This means that the individual could be in a different segment for different journeys, for example the regular business traveller, will also sometimes be a holiday–maker. But, for any particular journey the passenger will be in one segment only

■ in estate agency – domestic, commercial, industrial and retail. In this case the segments are identified by the different products which the customers are interested in

■ in catering – fast food, mainstream eating, specialist/ethnic, gourmet. In this case the segments are defined in terms of the quality of service expected by the customer

■ in the building trade – small, medium and large. In this instance the segments are defined by the scale and complexity of their requirements

■ in the food manufacturing business – the major segments would be institutional caterers, restaurants and retail/domestic, but the restaurant segment could probably be further segmented according to the groupings that we have already listed under catering. The segments here are defined by the nature of the customer's business

The criterion used for identifying the segments is different in each of these examples; but what they have in common is that the customer can be in only one segment at any one time. As long as that condition is satisfied it is possible for companies to make a different provision for each segment and to charge different prices in each.

ACTION POINT 18

1. What market segment or product would you describe your product or service being in?

2. Does your company embrace more than one segment of the market. How does it do this?

8.1 THE ECONOMIC BASIS OF SEGMENTATION

An alternative way of explaining segmentation starts from basic economics

The law of demand

For any particular goods, the lower the price the more the consumer will want to buy, and vice versa

This relationship between price and demand can be shown as a 'demand curve', as thus

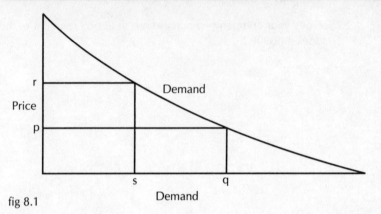

fig 8.1

At price **p** the quantity demanded will be **q**. At the higher price of **r** the quantity demand will be the lower amount **s**. The curve shows all the possible combinations of price and quantity.

The curve may be more or less steep, and more or less curved, but its general direction will always be from top left to bottom right.

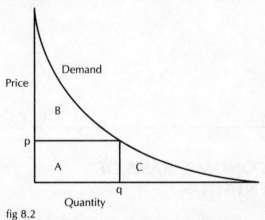

fig 8.2

If I sell at a single price **p** the customers will buy **q** and I will get a revenue of **p x q** (price x quantity), which is shown by the area A on the diagram. However, every buyer, except the last marginal one, was willing to pay more than **p**. The area under the curve **B** represents the additional amount of money which the buyers were willing to pay, but they did not need to, because the price p was the same for everyone.

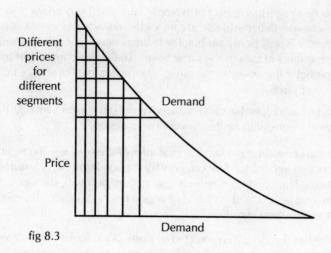

fig 8.3

If it were possible to make a separate deal with each individual, to get from each the maximum that they were willing to pay, then it would be possible to earn revenue of **A + B** for the same quantity sold.

Likewise, the area **C** represents potential revenue waiting to come your way, if you were able to lower your price, and if you had more to sell.

Using this model you can view customer segmentation as a tactic to charge a range of prices which follow the demand curve and which therefore extract more of the available revenue from the market.

Since no customer willingly pays more than they have to for a product, the seller who wishes to charge differential prices has to erect 'barriers' to prevent the higher paying customer from slipping down into a lower price bracket.

8.2 'NATURAL' AND 'FORCED' SEGMENTATION

From the story so far you will have realised that the term 'market segmentation' covers a number of practices which are quite different in their impact upon the customer

■   it may be based upon giving extra value or service for a higher price. The aim is to create products which are distinct enough to occupy separate markets eg. holiday and business hotels

■   it may be based upon privileges made available only to powerful customers in order to retain their business. Customers with less bargaining power (leverage) pay more. For example, cars sold for company fleets are much cheaper than the identical cars sold to individual buyers. The price differential is only partly attributable to the economies of scale in selling large numbers of cars to the same buyer. The major component in the differential is the power of the buyer. The higher level of service comes at a lower price

■ it may be based upon barriers contrived by the seller to prevent high price customers from slipping into lower price categories

Rail and air travel are the most familiar examples of these, where the business traveller is locked into the top fare category by the conditions which surround the lower fares. The conditions, which restrict time of travel, days of travel, advance booking period, and option to change a reservation, are all designed to keep out the business traveller.

The lower the fare the more it is protected by restrictions, so that the cost to the company of processing the fares actually goes up as the fares go down.

This kind of segmentation is frequently operated alongside the first kind, which offers a higher level of service for a higher price. The two are liable to become confused in the minds of the customers, who are not always sure whether they are paying a high price for a more comfortable seat or for travelling on a Monday morning. In fact the higher price is not for one or the other, but for one added to the other.

The segmentation which uses what we have called 'contrived barriers' is typically resented by those customers who have to pay the higher price. The hostility of London commuters towards British Rail is a well known example of this.

8.3 FINDING A NICHE

It is possible, of course, for a business to go for one specialised segment of the market and try to establish an unassailable position for itself in that segment. This policy has come to be known as 'niche marketing'.

The idea of the 'niche ' has been borrowed from animal and plant ecology, where it is used to describe the way some species have evolved to survive in very specialised habitats, or niches. The polar bear, for example, has no competitor or enemy within their very severe, Arctic environment.

In the typical business niche the company that gets there first can establish such a dominant position with the customers that it is not worth the effort of any other company to try to get in. Specialised trade publications would be a good example of this. The ambition of most such publications is to become the 'industry bible', so that readers and advertisers do not even think of using any other publication.

What distinguishes a niche from a monopoly is that there are no legal protections, regulations, or physical constraints which would prevent a competitor from entering the market. The only barrier to entry is the cost of establishing a position from scratch against a business which is already established.

Whoever occupies a niche needs to be constantly anticipating potential competition and taking action to prevent it from emerging. The niche company has to be careful not to over–exploit its position. The customers have to feel that they are getting value for money. As soon as they feel they are being exploited they will start looking for alternatives. In effect, they will invite in the competition.

The niche occupier also needs to keep a close watch on developments in the business of its customers. In particular it needs to look out for the emergence of groups that may become new niches within the larger niche. When these groups grow large enough they could break away and transfer their custom to a new competitor.

For example, if you were producing a 'niche publication' for the catering and hotel trade, you would naturally be aware of the growth of fast food outlets, take–aways, and pub catering.

Are you going to provide articles and advertising in your current publication to retain or attract this readership?

Are you going to produce periodic supplements or inserts for these groups?

Are you going to set up completely separate publications for them?

Or are you going to allow your competitors a free run with these new groups while you concentrate on retaining your existing, mainstream customers.

8.4 PERISHABLE SERVICES

When we were looking at the demand curve we saw that there was an element of potential revenue available from people who were prepared to buy, but only at a lower price than was being asked.

This is represented by the area C on the diagram.

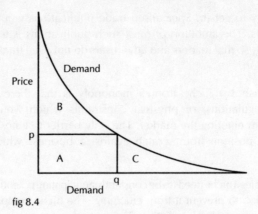

fig 8.4

If you are producing goods that can be stored on a shelf you would normally prefer to store them than to sell them for less than the going rate. However if you are producing services, such as transport, entertainment, education, consultancy, hairdressing, or hotel accommodation, you cannot store your product. If it is not consumed at the time that it is produced then it is simply wasted.

An empty seat in the theatre after the show has begun is bringing in no money at all. It was worth £20, but suddenly it is worthless. Any revenue you could get for it would be better than nothing.

A good deal of ingenuity goes into attracting extra revenue for the 'spare' capacity which would otherwise perish. The ingenuity is directed at ensuring that it is additional revenue drawn from area C on the diagram, and not a transfer, from area A, which is revenue that would have been received anyway.

There are various tactics used to ensure you do not 'dilute' the existing revenue when you sell your spare capacity at reduced price

■   confine the reduction to supposed low income groups, who can produce evidence of status: students, pensioners, claimants

■   make the conditions so stringent that only the very cost–conscious customer would tolerate them

■   control capacity so that the customer for the stand–by special rate has to take a chance on not getting what they want

The conditions are designed to make sure that the full–rate customer is not tempted into the reduced rate market. They are not designed to humiliate the reduced rate customer.

It is a fundamental principle of customer service that once the reduced rate customer has got over the various hurdles that have been placed in their path they are treated exactly the same as any other customer/passenger/guest.

CHAPTER SUMMARY

Having completed this chapter you should now

■ understand the basic principles of market segmentation

■ know the difference between natural and forced segmentation

■ be aware of the niche markets

■ know what is meant by perishable services

If you are unsure about any of these areas, go back and re-read the relevant part(s) of the text.

9 LIVING WITH CHANGE

There is plenty of talking and writing about change, as though it were something peculiar to our time. One of the popular clichés on the subject is the claim those of us alive today are experiencing more change than any previous generation; although it is never made very clear what 'more change' means. An equally strong case could be made that the years 1910–1930 saw more change than 1970–1990. But the argument is pointless.

No one doubts that there is plenty of change happening, and it is probably true that on a global scale more people than ever before are experiencing profound changes in their work, their relationships and their lifestyles. Indeed, there are more people on earth than ever before, and that in itself is a major driving force of change.

9.1 PREDICTABLE CHANGES

From the perspective of our own society what seems different about the present time from most of what has gone before, is not so much that change is ever present as that people expect it to be a continuing factor in their lives. There is no longer a general expectation that we will 'return to normal' when we have, beaten inflation, achieved full employment, ended the cold war, stabilised exchange rates, integrated road and rail transport and so on and on. No one now believes, if they ever did, that stability lies on the other side of all these desirable objectives. There will just be more change and different change.

We know that the future will be different, and that we will be part of that difference. This chapter tries to piece together what we know and what we can reasonably predict about the future. The aim is to reduce, if possible, the amount of shock and surprise which the future holds. The more we know about the future, the better prepared we shall be, and the more in control of our own affairs. Being prepared is what is often called being lucky; usually by onlookers who are unaware of the groundwork which has gone into a successful enterprise. It can take as long as 20 years to become an 'overnight success'.

Preparing for predictable change is not about letting your imagination run riot. In the optimism of the 1960s, anticipating the 'white heat of the technological revolution' that was reputedly on the horizon, there were plenty of predictions being made of how we would be living in the 1990s.

COLLEGE OF MARKETING LIBRARY AND DESIGN

How many of you now work a two day week? have your own private flying machines? have your cooking and housework done by voice–activated robots?

and take holidays on the moon?

Not a very good hit rate for the more imaginative futurologists of thirty years ago.

What was really difficult to imagine in 1961 was how similar life would turn out to be in 1991; and that thought should remind us that we already know much more about the future than we might suppose. What we know falls into four categories

Irreversabilities

There are many things currently in existence, or projects under way, that cannot be undone.

The number of 20 year olds in 10 years time cannot exceed the number of 10 year olds today. The Channel Tunnel will be carrying rail traffic in 1994. The average temperature of the world will rise.

Contingencies

These are things that will happen **unless some positive action is taken to prevent them**.

Road traffic congestion will increase. The cost of non–renewable energy resources will increase. An increasing number of pensioners will be supported by a diminishing number of people in work.

Durables

Some things will not be much affected by change.

Human nature will probably continue much as before, along with all the institutions founded upon it. The nuclear family will be around for a long time. People will continue to seek security, the esteem of others, and some freedom to express themselves.

Safe bets

Some current trends still have plenty of momentum.

Data–processing and communications equipment will continue its trend of becoming cheaper and more powerful. 'Green' issues, energy conservation, and the protection of the environment, will became more important in national and international politics. Service and knowledge–based industries will grow much faster than manufacturing.

All the information which we have used as examples in these four categories is common knowledge. None of the examples will have surprised anyone; but even these rather obvious insights have huge implications for the future of nearly all businesses.

In the rest of this chapter we shall look at what is happening now, and what we can reasonably expect to happen in the future, in four areas of concern for business. These are

■   technology

■   trade and industry

■   people

■   organisations

In each of these areas we shall look particularly at the impact which the changes might have on the relationship between organisations and their clients.

9.2   TECHNOLOGY

About ten years ago there was a widespread expectation among people in the know that new developments in biology would be the source of the most important changes in industry and in our daily lives. We are still waiting for the wonder drugs, the inexhaustible sources of nourishing protein, and the environmentally friendly pesticides and fertilizers.

With hindsight it is easy to see that our hopes for bio–technology were pinned upon expected breakthroughs. But the very nature of a breakthrough is that it is a low–probability event. Calling a low–probability event that has not yet happened a 'breakthrough' is a tactic for attracting money, not an objective appraisal. Anyone who puts up the money had better think of it as a gamble rather than an investment.

Meanwhile the really profound changes in the way we do business were brought about by a technology which was advancing steadily by small increments. Microelectronics, as applied to communication systems, to information processing, and to the control of machinery (formerly 'automation' now 'robotics'), has affected every area of work, home and leisure activities. The trend has been for the components, whether they are mainframe computers, micro chips, telephone exchanges or CD players, to become smaller, more powerful, cheaper and more programmable, in the sense of giving the user more choice and control in operating the equipment.

ACTION POINT 19

What effect has technology had on your working practices during the last five years?

The effects of these trends reinforce one another. It is likely that all four of them will continue; but even if only one of them continues we could still expect to see in the future even more of the following

■ more employees coming on–line to their company's computer network, and having direct and immediate access to information

■ easier communications between systems

■ more interactivity ie. it will be easier for the users to interrogate and instruct computerised systems

We could expect all of these trends to have the following effects

- more decision–making will be in the hands of the staff who are on–line, and have the information they need to make decisions

- more information will be accessible to all departments in a company. There will be fewer secrets

- companies and customers will be linked by communication networks which will enable them to exchange information, place orders, transfer funds and synchronise their plans as easily as if they were the same organisation

- company departments and individuals can be widely dispersed. They will not need to be physically close to communicate effectively with each other, or to act on behalf of the company with the outside world

9.3   TRADE AND INDUSTRY

There were a number of structural changes in the patterns of trade and industry that gave the decade of the 80s its distinctive flavour. We can expect to continue to feel their effects into the foreseeable future.

Deregulation and Competition

The withdrawal of governments from the control and protection of certain industries, and the encouragement of competition in general: these are policies most closely associated in this country with the name of Mrs Thatcher. But throughout the 80s similar policies were being implemented in countries as diverse in their politics and traditions as France, Australia and Mexico.

In this country financial services, shipbuilding, air transport, bus services, telecommunications, radio and television, and high street opticians, to mention just a few, were all more or less opened up to competition. Now, even the countries of Eastern Europe are following suit.

This worldwide policy shift was partly in recognition of the increasing political importance of consumers relative to producers. Consumers in general were no longer willing to bear the cost of supporting industries which often seemed to be doing very little to help themselves. The policy was also intended to help British companies to compete on the international scene. Other countries would not tolerate competition from companies that were protected from competition in their own home market.

Globalisation

Companies increasingly operate on a world–wide scale. Even relatively small companies now see the whole world or at least the whole of Europe as their market. For many highly specialised companies one single country cannot provide a sufficient market to keep them going.

At the same time large companies are spreading themselves around the world, not just selling their products in other countries but setting up, or buying up, production facilities. Increasingly goods are produced anywhere for sale anywhere. The name on the label gives no clue to where it was made. Sony TVs may come from Wales, Philips radios may come from Brazil.

Consumers all over the world seem to be prepared to buy the same things. Levi jeans, Coca Cola, Big Macs, Gucci shoes, Benetton sweaters, can all be brought in identical form throughout the world using the same credit card.

The Growth of Service and Knowledge–Based Businesses

Most of the low–tech manufacturing industry has disappeared from this country and from other 'developed' countries. For the most part it has shifted to poorer, developing countries where labour is cheaper. In so far as it has been replaced it is with service and knowledge–based industries, to the point where these have the majority of employees in most developed countries.

Some services, by their very nature have to be produced at the same place as they are consumed. Transport, catering, entertainment, health–care, retailing, cannot be produced overseas and imported, so we can safely assume that they will continue to be major employers in this country. However, much of their work is low in technology, low in skill and low in pay.

The knowledge–based industries, like financial services, telecommunications, news and entertainment media, computer software, and various kinds of professional services, are for the most part high–tech, highly skilled and highly paid. Most of these businesses could, in principle, be located anywhere, and distribute their services to their customers using the same high technology that helped to create them in the first place.

All our radio and television could be cabled in from Luxembourg. All the deregulated financial services concentrated in the City of London could be carried out in Frankfurt, with London as a satellite. Our newspapers could be written and typeset in Paris and faxed to the UK for local printing and distribution.

The knowledge–based industries are the top end of the service sector. This is where the serious skills are used and the serious money is made, and that is why they are under constant threat from competition. The competition can only increase, and for this reason, they need to have their customers on their side.

These are high risk – high reward businesses. They have very few assets apart from the confidence and loyalty of their customers, and they do not own these but have them on loan. If their customers feel that they are being exploited, kept in the dark or taken for granted then they will be receptive to a better offer. If they get a better offer they can desert en masse almost overnight.

With the benefit of hindsight everyone will see that the losers had it coming to them.

9.4 PEOPLE

'The fundamentals still apply, as time goes by'. The song got it right. When we were looking at what we already know about the future we put human nature, the basic motives which move people to action, into the category of 'durables'.

However, the ways in which they express these basic motives are liable to vary according to how secure they feel, how well they think they understand what is happening around them, their experience of the past, and their expectations of the future. All of these factors are leading in a similar direction. In the future you can expect your staff, your colleagues and your customers to be wiser, greyer and greener.

Wiser

People are staying on longer at school. More people are going on to further education, full time and part–time. More people are working for recognised technical and professional qualifications.

At the same time the entry requirement for jobs is rising; so that it is increasingly difficult for people without some further education or formal qualification to get a job at all.

The cause and affect relationship between these two trends is not straightforward. Many jobs are now given entry requirements higher than is strictly necessary to do them, because the applicants are now better qualified anyway. Raising the entry level is an expedient way of keeping the number of applicants down to a manageable level. Nonetheless, for all the reasons which we have already discussed, the jobs that have a future do require people who are technically competent, able to make their own decisions, and able to deal with people.

The new employees expect change. They expect to be continually relearning their jobs, and to be allowed the training, the time and the facilities for doing so. They expect to be used more effectively, and not to have their time or their abilities wasted by unimaginative supervision and controls. They expect less job security and higher rewards.

The National Curriculum in schools has introduced a much larger element of exploration and discovery, and learning how to learn. The price of this is that there is less emphasis on acquiring a predetermined subject matter, or on learning facts as against skills. The intention is that people will emerge from the education system equipped to continue learning and to cope with change. The effects of this will serve only to reinforce the trends which we have already noted.

Greyer

The population of this country, and of the developed world in general is going to get older over the next 20 years. The Economist's survey of 1991 summarises it thus

> 'By 2000 one in three West Europeans will be over 50. In Germany the percentage of people of this age will rise from 27% to 37%. In Italy from 23% to 33%. Only a little less in France and Britain. Before the end of the century, these people will inhabit something like 35% of all the houses in Western Europe'.

This is the generation of what was called the post–war bulge in Europe, closely followed by the baby–boom in the USA, working its way through the system.

More of the women of this generation will return to work, if they are not working already. And because of the decreasing numbers of school leavers available over the next decade, the generation of men who found that they were 'too old at forty five', in the shakedowns of the 1980s, may find that they are 'just the job at fifty five'.

A more affluent, more secure and more assertive middle–aged generation could become a major influence in how we work and what we produce in the 1990s. These people are the generation which formed their ideas in the 1960s and often think of themselves as more radical and adventurous than their own children. As consumers they will not conform to the 'old fogey' image which is still popular with advertisers aiming at this age group. To quote the Economist again: 'Many of these people will go to their graves still humming 'Jumpin' Jack Flash'.

Greener

A concern for the 'quality of life' was once confined to an intellectual minority who felt themselves to be crying in the wilderness. Indeed, preserving the wilderness was one of their objectives.

One of the major shifts of the late 1980s was the realisation that this concerned everyone, and the adoption of green concerns by all the major political parties and all the news media. Concerns about the pollution of the environment, the depletion of our resources, the over–exploitation of land and water, the worldwide accumulation of waste products, the degeneration of public places and some public services, will not go away.

Once people have been alerted to the problem they begin to see evidence of it all around them, and their increased awareness reinforces their concern. These issues are likely to become more rather than less important in the future as more people begin to feel that time is not on our side.

We can expect that companies will be put under closer scrutiny by the public at large and by their customers. They will be expected not only to deliver the goods and services but also to accept responsibility for the environment which they work in and which they create.

Companies are already legally accountable to their shareholders for their financial balance sheet and profit and loss. In a parallel and informal way they will increasingly find themselves accountable to their customers and to their neighbours for their environmental balance sheet and profit and loss account.

There is already a very visible increase in the number of consumer products which are recycled, recyclable, bio–degradable, ozone–friendly and so on. The industries which have been most criticised, like oil, chemicals, energy, and motor manufacturing, have all launched advertising campaigns which emphasis their contribution to conservation and to controlling the unwanted side–effects of their products.

It is, of course, possible to take a cynical view of all this, and see it as window–dressing and lip service on the part of the business community. But it is at least a recognition that a company's reputation depends upon more than just the performance of the products which it sells.

Most companies have not begun to realise what this might mean for them in the future. If they treat it as a threat and go on the defensive they are likely to lose the battle for the hearts and minds of their customers. If they treat it as an opportunity to create new partnerships with their customers and the public they could secure their position as 'pillars of the community'.

ACTION POINT 20

Comment on the effects environment issues have had on your company.

9.5 ORGANISATIONS

In response to the pressures of technology, of competition, and of customer and employee expectations, we can expect to see some changes in the way organisations are structured and managed. Some of these changes are already with us, some have been promised but are a long time coming. At their best they attempt to reconcile efficiency in methods with increased choice and more satisfying work for the individual employee. At the worst they attempt to copy the Japanese in the hope that some of their charisma will rub off on us.

Expect to see organisations become flatter, more flexible, and networked.

Flatter

In the recession of the late 70s and early 80s many companies shed large numbers of staff and made it their objective to reduce the number of levels in their organisations.

Middle management and supervisors of supervisors were going to be squeezed out. Senior managers would communicate more directly with front line staff. Front line staff would be given more elbow room to use their intelligence and discretion.

In the event, many companies managed to reduce staff numbers at all levels, including management and supervision; but, in spite of their intentions, they finished up with the same number of levels as they had before.

The recession of the late 80s early 90s has brought a second wave of staff cuts and restructuring to many of the same companies who thought they had gone through it for the last time ten years ago. What seems to be different about this latest shakedown is that it has affected management levels more than other levels of employees. This time a number of large companies really will reduce the number of levels in their organisations.

What has made the difference is that information technology has at last fulfilled its promise (or carried out its threat, depending on you point of view). In the intervening period many of the functions previously carried out by middle management have been bundled into a box and are now carried out without any visible human intervention.

Passing on routine information, authorising spending, scheduling work, checking work, generating standard reports; all of these are typical of the kind of predictable, recurring and rule–governed activities which therefore come into the general category of the programmable. As computer technology becomes faster, cheaper, smaller and more accessible to the lay person, more and more of the potentially programmable activities of the organisation are actually being programmed.

Which leaves the management function stripped down to its essentials of making the non–routine, non–programmable decisions, providing leadership and purpose to the organisation, and developing its assets – in particular its staff and its customers. These activities rely more on the quality than the quantity of management.

The flattening of organisations will have some interesting consequences for careers. There will be fewer rungs on the organisational ladder, so the people who make it will to the top will get there faster, and stay there longer. But there will be fewer places at the top, and fewer places on the intermediate rungs, so there will be less movement in total 'up the ladder'. Fewer people can expect to make progress in that way. The ladder will no longer be an appropriate symbol, and we shall have to describe career progress in some other terms.

It should be possible to add value to oneself in the organisation by adding more abilities and becoming more versatile; or by becoming more skilled and authoritative within ones chosen specialism. It may even be accepted eventually that managing or supervising is only one of many ways of contributing to the success of an organisation, and that the many ways are no better or worse than one other, just different.

As far as the customers are concerned, the main impact of the flattened organisation on them is that they are likely to see more of the senior members of the organisation, since there will be fewer intermediaries to get over and round before they meet the real boss. By the same token they should find that decisions are made and problems solved more quickly.

ACTION POINT 21

Has the trend of 'flattening' affected the organisation of your company? If so, how?

Flexible

The flexible organisation is one that can expand and contract itself to match variations in demand.

Whether the variations are seasonal, cyclical, or random, businesses that are subject to wide variations in demand have always been faced with a dilemma. If they maintain levels of staffing and other resources sufficient to meet the peaks in demand then they will be paying for unproductive resources during the troughs. If they maintain resource levels only sufficient to meet low or average demand then they will be turning away business at peak times.

There are various ways of getting around this dilemma. If

- the level of demand in general is on a rising trend
- it is possible to accumulate stocks in the lean times to sell in the good times
- staff and other resources costs are low
- you are able to pass your unproductive costs on to the customer

you could survive in a fluctuating markets even if you carried a surplus capacity for most of the time. However, in the 1990s fewer and fewer companies are able to satisfy any of these conditions.

They are therefore looking for ways in which the organisation can be expanded and contracted at short notice, and this involves developing new kinds of working relationships which offer a number of alternatives to the traditional employer/employee contract.

The flexible organisation is liable to be a combination of any or all of the following

1   a permanent team of managers who keep in close touch with the customers, monitor their requirements, and make plans as far ahead as they are able. This group provides the continuity of the organisation

2   a permanent core of professional, technical and support people sufficient to handle only the minimum level of demand. These people may be multi–skilled and 'flexible' in their own right, but they would be employees in the traditional sense

3   a group of skilled people whom the company undertakes to use for a certain number of days each year, at the company's choice. These people therefore have a guaranteed income from the company. They can add to this income, if they choose, by working on a similar basis for other organisations, or doing other completely unrelated work

4   a further group of people known to be competent, who are used on a
         casual of freelance basis

Groups 3 and 4 would be self–employed. Group 3 is paid a higher daily rate than
they would get if they were full–time employees; but since they have an assured
level of income from the company they are not paid as much per day as the
freelancers in Group 4.

This pattern or organisation can be visualised as concentric circles, rather than
as the conventional pyramid.

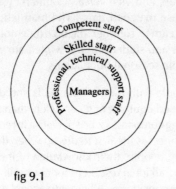

fig 9.1

Many companies have offered short–term consultancy work to redundant
executives as a way of softening the blow of redundancy; but that is a long way
short of the flexible organisation structure that we have just described.

Although the flexible organisation is still radical and rare in manufacturing and
service businesses it has in fact been around for a very long time in other areas,
It has always been the norm in the music–making business, in television
programme–making, in newspaper publishing, in some areas of adult education
and in mini–cab operations.

Most of these existing examples are in the category that we have been calling
knowledge–based businesses and that is not a coincidence. The increase in
flexible structures will follow the expected increase in knowledge–based
industries, but other kinds of industries will be tempted to try it too.

As more companies operate flexible structures it becomes easier for all of them
to do so. Because, as we have said, it is the norm in the music business, it is
possible for a freelance musician to make a good living getting regular work
from several different full–time orchestras, working as a session musician in
recording studios, augmenting amateur orchestras, running his or her own
small group, and teaching. The industry is geared up to making this kind of mix–

and–match lifestyle possible, with a supporting structure of agents, concert promoters, trade press and informal networks of contacts.

Other industries have a long way to go to establish the kind of formal and informal processes that enable this kind of specialised labour market to operate. But it is not, in principle, difficult to do it.

A neat alternative, which is available to some businesses that are subject to fluctuating demand, is to develop a second–string product whose demand is inversely related to the demand for the first–string product. As the one goes down the other goes up, and vice versa. 'Counter–cyclical' businesses is the technical term for these matched pairs. The man who sweeps chimneys in winter and sells ice cream in summer, the boarding house that takes holiday–makers in the summer and students in the winter, are very basic examples of coping with predictable seasonal fluctuations.

If a company has people with transferable skills and does not have a heavy investment in specialised equipment it can often change direction overnight. For example, consulting companies who specialise in recruitment and selection can find that their business is the first to dry up when there is a recession; but their skills in assessing people, their knowledge of the job market and their network of contacts are all ideal resources for counselling employees about to be made redundant, or considering whether to accept a severance offer. Many large accounting firms are currently riding a boom in managing insolvencies. This more than compensates for the decline in their work on new business start-ups.

Once again knowledge–based businesses are the ones which can most easily make the kind of switch we have described. With the increase in such businesses, more and more of them will be looking for opportunities to complement and counterbalance their main line of activity with a fall–back or second line. Ideally the alternative services will be produced for the same set of customers, wearing different hats so to speak.

Most second string businesses are, in fact, set up at the suggestion of customers who find they have a need for a different kind of service and would prefer to use people they already know. If your customers have developed a confidence in you in a general sense, and not simply as a specialist in what you happen to be doing at the moment, they will develop your business for you.

Networked

The use of the word 'networking' was made popular in the early 80s by Rank Xerox who used it to describe their method of putting some of their executives on a part–time consulting contract and giving them computers and modems so that they could work from home. That kind of networking was a pioneering attempt in the UK to create the kind of flexible organisation structure that we have just described.

However, when we talk of networking in this chapter we mean something on a much more ambitious scale. We mean the use of computer links to integrate the activities of chains of suppliers, producers, distributors and retailers so that they form a seamless whole. They may be separate businesses, but from the point of view of the customer they act as if they were one business.

The best–established example of this is the airline business, where world–wide networks enable Travel Agents to make bookings and issue tickets on any flights. The customer has access to all the world's airlines from any on–line retail outlet. The so–called 'big bang' of 1985 introduced a similar integration into the world–wide market for many kind of financial services.

The practice of networking is now extending into manufacturing. Manufacturing companies are increasingly adopting Just–in–Time techniques of production scheduling, to eliminate the cost of holding stocks of parts. The Economist reports that companies who supply parts to the motor industry are 'building factories next door to their big customers' assembly plants and then linking their computers. In this way they can roll parts off their production line and straight into their customers' factories. By eliminating inventory, this makes the value of their parts hard to compare with even the fiercest off–site rivals.'

As the quote from the Economist implies, when companies establish this kind of integration they both gain an advantage, but they have also established a form of partnership and commitment to each other which effectively rules out the possibility of the customer shopping around, or of the supplier going over to the competition. The customer may also use other suppliers, and the supplier may also supply competitor companies; but this does not alter the fact that they now have an important stake in each others business. Neither side can afford to let the other down.

You may have noticed one peculiar consequence of networking as we have described it. In its application to services, like airlines and finance, it is about widening choice to the customer; and it has a tendency to reduce the products to a commodity. In the application to manufacturing it is about saving time. Here it has the effect of giving particular suppliers a privileged position, and raising what might otherwise be a commodity to the status of a differentiated product.

In both cases these side–effects, as you might call them, are undesirable for one set of people. The service suppliers lose some of their identity in exchange for access to the market, the manufacturing customers lose their freedom to chose suppliers in exchange for an assurance of continuity and quality of supply. Clearly the advantages must outweigh the disadvantages or they would not be doing it.

If the trends to globalisation of markets and increasing competition continues we can expect that the relative advantages of both kinds of networking will increase.

CHAPTER SUMMARY

Having completed this chapter you should now

- ■ be aware that change is inevitable

- ■ know the changes which have taken place on the technological front in recent years

- ■ be aware of the changes which have affected industry over the last 30 years

- ■ understand our increase in the knowledge in recent years

- ■ know the effects that all these factors have had on organisations, their structure and culture

- ■ understand the meaning of networking in the organisational context

If you are unsure about any of these areas, go back and re-read the relevant part(s) of the text.

COLLEGE OF MARKETING LIBRARY AND DESIGN